92
Roo   Greenblatt, Miriam

Franklin D. Roosevelt

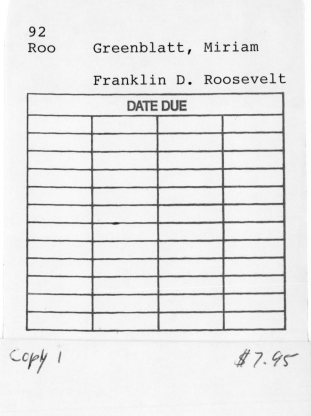

DATE DUE			

Copy 1 $7.95

CHRIST METHODIST DAY SCHOOL
LIBRARY

Franklin D. Roosevelt

32nd President of the United States

The only President to be re-elected to a third and later a fourth term, Franklin D. Roosevelt rekindled the confidence of the American people in themselves and in democracy, both at home and abroad. (Library of Congress.)

Franklin D. Roosevelt

32nd President of the United States

Miriam Greenblatt

CHRIST METHODIST DAY SCHOOL
LIBRARY

 GARRETT EDUCATIONAL CORPORATION

Cover: *Official presidential portrait of Franklin D. Roosevelt by Frank O. Salisbury.* (Copyrighted by the White House Historical Association; photograph by the National Geographic Society.)

Copyright © 1989 by Miriam Greenblatt

All rights reserved including the right of reproduction in whole or in part in any form without the prior written permission of the publisher. Published by Garrett Educational Corporation, 130 East 13th Street, P.O. Box 1588, Ada, Oklahoma 74820.

Manufactured in the United States of America

Edited and produced by Synthegraphics Corporation

Library of Congress Cataloging in Publication Data

Greenblatt, Miriam.
    Franklin D. Roosevelt: 32nd President of the United States
    (Presidents of the United States)
    Bibliography: p.
    Includes index.
    Summary: Follows the life of the thirty-second president from birth to death, examining his childhood, education, employment, and political career.
    1. Roosevelt, Franklin D. (Franklin Delano), 1882–1945—Juvenile literature.   2. Presidents—United States—Biography—Juvenile literature.   [1. Roosevelt. Franklin D. (Franklin Delano), 1882–1945.   2. Presidents.]   I. Title.   Series.
E807.G696   1988   973.917'092'4—dc19   [B]   [92]
87-36121
ISBN 0-944483-06-2

Contents

Chronology for
Franklin D. Roosevelt

1882	Born on January 30 at Hyde Park, New York
1896-1900	Attended Groton School for Boys
1900-1904	Attended Harvard University
1904-1907	Attended Columbia University School of Law
1905	Married Anna Eleanor Roosevelt on March 17
1910-1913	Served as a senator in the New York state legislature
1913-1920	Served as assistant secretary of the navy
1920	Nominated for Vice-President but defeated in the election
1921	Stricken with infantile paralysis
1924	First visited Warm Springs, Georgia
1928-1932	Served as governor of New York
1932	Elected 32nd President of the United States
1936	Re-elected to a second term
1940	First President re-elected for a third term
1944	Re-elected for a fourth term
1945	Died on April 12 at Warm Springs, Georgia

Chapter 1

Early Years

The day was December 8, 1941. The time was 12:30 P.M. All across the United States — in classrooms, factories, offices, and homes — tens of millions of Americans sat in front of radios, listening to President Franklin Delano Roosevelt address an emergency session of Congress. His warm, resonant voice rang out:

> Yesterday, December 7, 1941 — a date which will live in infamy — the United States of America was attacked by naval and air forces of the Empire of Japan. . . . No matter how long it may take us to overcome this unpremeditated invasion, the American people, in their righteous might, will win through to absolute victory. . . . Hostilities exist. There is no blinking at the fact that our people, our territory, and our interests are in grave danger. With confidence in our armed forces — with the unbounded determination of our people — we will gain the inevitable triumph — so help us God.

The entire speech took only six minutes. When the President finished, Congress declared war on Japan, and the United States entered World War II.

More than 8½ years earlier, on March 4, 1933, President Roosevelt had delivered another speech to which the entire nation listened. As in 1941, the United States faced a crisis. It was in the midst of the Great Depression, when one out of every four workers was without a job, when millions of families had lost all their savings, when thousands of homeless people slept on park benches, and when the future looked very grim.

Then, too, Roosevelt had described both the difficulties confronting the country and his unwavering belief that the American people would triumph over them. Then, as in 1941, he had sounded a clarion call to action: "This great nation will endure as it has endured, will revive and will prosper. . . . Let me assert my firm belief that the only thing we have to fear is fear itself."

In both 1933 and 1941, Franklin Delano Roosevelt helped lead the American people to victory. No other 20th-century President has had so great an impact on his country and on the world.

COUNTRY LIFE

Franklin Delano Roosevelt was born on January 30, 1882, in Hyde Park, a town in Dutchess County, New York. His father, James Roosevelt, noted the event in his wife's diary as follows: "At a quarter to nine my Sallie [officially, her name was Sara] had a splendid large baby boy. He weighs ten pounds without clothes." Franklin was to be his parents' only child.

The Roosevelt family was part of New York's aristocracy. James Roosevelt was a wealthy man who had been an executive of several coal mining and railroad companies. By the time Franklin was born, however, James had more or less retired to an estate overlooking the Hudson River. There, he raised trotting horses and carried on experiments to improve the soil and grow new plants.

The family home at Hyde Park—now a national historic site—was a spacious, rambling, wooden-sided house. The large household staff included maids, cooks, coachmen, gardeners, and farmhands, as well as a governess for Franklin.

In addition to being a working farm, Hyde Park was a delightful place in which to grow up. It had beautiful gardens and lawns, sweet-smelling meadows to run through, and acres of woodland to explore. There were ponies to ride and dogs with which to play. In summer, Franklin rowed and canoed on the Hudson River. In winter, when the river froze solidly from shore to shore, he went skating and iceboating. He also liked tobogganing down the long hill behind the house.

Franklin's boyhood horizons were not limited to Hyde Park. In summer, the family usually went to its summer estate on Campobello Island off the coast of Maine. There, Franklin learned to love the sea. He also learned how to swim and how to sail the 51-foot family yacht, the *Half Moon*. Eventually he received his own 21-footer, the *New Moon*.

In winter, the Roosevelt family usually spent several weeks in New York City. While his parents paid social calls and attended the theater and the opera, Franklin practically lived at the American Museum of Natural History. He was so fascinated by the museum's extensive bird collection that he decided to make a collection of his own. At the age of 10, he began shooting one of each kind of bird he could find in Dutchess County. He would then mount the bird in a glass-fronted case that his parents allowed him to keep in the downstairs hall. He was very careful, though, never to kill a bird during the nesting season.

Franklin became interested in collecting other things besides birds. He especially enjoyed model ships and anything to do with the U.S. Navy. But of all his hobbies, stamp collecting was probably his favorite. It not only provided much pleasure but also taught him a great deal about geography. By the time Franklin was elected President of the United States, his stamp collection was world famous.

THE EDUCATION OF AN ARISTOCRAT

Franklin's main companion during his childhood was his father. Every day after breakfast, they would go out to look over the farm, examine the newborn animals, and help clean out the pens and stables. James would explain to his son how important it was to conserve land, trees, and water.

Franklin also accompanied his father to board meetings of charitable and educational organizations. As a member of the aristocracy, James Roosevelt believed strongly that people with wealth and position had an obligation to help those who were less fortunate. When Franklin grew up, he would be expected to perform similar duties.

Among the other things that Franklin learned from his father was to treat the poorer children of Hyde Park as his equals, not his inferiors. He also learned that it was necessary to resist tyranny. That idea had a foundation in experience: as a young man, James Roosevelt had fought with Giuseppi Garibaldi to free Italy from foreign control and form a nation out of the divided Italian states.

Franklin's upbringing was also influenced by his mother. Sara Roosevelt was very organized; she planned her son's days just as she planned the household duties for the servants. Hours were set aside for study, for play, for visiting relatives, and for doing other things. Although Franklin sometimes rebelled at being so organized, he generally agreed with his mother that "the greatest fun is to get things done."

Sara Roosevelt also taught her son to enjoy good literature. Franklin spent many a long winter evening listening to his mother read aloud—history, biography, fiction, and especially the Bible. His favorite author was Mark Twain.

Still another thing that Franklin learned from his mother was the importance of good manners. All his relatives found him extremely charming and well-behaved. He was also quite skillful at getting what he wanted from the adults around him.

Franklin with his parents at Hyde Park when he was nine years old. When Franklin was born, his father was 53 years old and his mother was 27 years old. Franklin was named after one of his mother's favorite uncles. (Franklin D. Roosevelt Library.)

Tutors and Travel

Between the ages of six and 14, Franklin—like many other well-to-do youngsters in the Hudson Valley—was tutored at home. In addition to French and German, he studied Latin, mathematics, penmanship, and ancient history. But Franklin especially enjoyed reading about ships and the men who sailed them. When he grew up, he often thought, he would like to be an officer in the U.S. Navy.

Franklin's early education included frequent trips with his parents to Europe. The most memorable trip took place in 1896. While James Roosevelt was taking treatments at the baths at Nauheim, Germany, Franklin was enrolled in a local school. It was an unpleasant experience for the young American. German students were supposed only to listen to their teacher and never ask questions. They were expected to stand, sit, and walk in unison. To Franklin, it was like being in the army.

Franklin's dislike for German life was reinforced by a bicycle trip he took during a school holiday. He and his tutor were arrested four times in a single day! Their "crimes" included picking cherries from a branch that hung over the road, accidentally knocking over a goose, wheeling their bicycles into a railroad station, and entering a walled city after sundown. Everywhere they went, it seemed to Franklin, there was a sign saying *Verboten* — forbidden. "The law of this country is— Forbidden to breathe," he commented. He couldn't wait to return to the United States. "I now understand what it means to be free."

Going to Groton

In the fall of 1896, at the age of 14, Franklin entered the Groton School for boys, a college preparatory school located in the countryside about 35 miles north of Boston. Groton was a very exclusive school. First of all, because the annual tuition was $500, a large sum in those days, you had to be rich to attend. Second, you had to come from a socially prominent family. And third, you had to have been registered from infancy. The only thing that distinguished Franklin from his schoolmates was the fact that, like his father, he was a Democrat rather than a Republican.

A Strict Environment

Groton had been founded by the Reverend Endicott Peabody, an Episcopal clergyman who believed that the purpose of education was to turn out gentlemen and scholars of "mainly Christian character." Accordingly, he modeled Groton after such famous English boarding schools as Eton and Harrow.

Living conditions at Groton were very simple. Each boy slept in a cubicle about six feet wide and nine feet long. In addition to a narrow bed, the cubicle contained a bureau, a chair, and a small rug. Because there was no closet, Franklin had to hang his suits on pegs on the wall. There was no door, only a cloth curtain, because Dr. Peabody did not believe in privacy for students.

Boys at Groton were expected to rise, take a cold shower with yellow laundry soap in the common bathroom, dress, and be ready for breakfast by 7:30. After breakfast, they attended chapel. Classes began at 8:30, stopped at noon for lunch, and then continued until late afternoon. They were followed by athletic activities in which everyone, regardless of their interest or skill, had to take part. Playing football and baseball, Dr. Peabody believed, helped make you "a manly fellow."

Boys dressed for dinner in a dark suit, a white shirt with a stiffly starched collar, and black patent leather evening shoes. The meal was followed by a second chapel service and a study period. Then the boys would shake hands with Dr. and Mrs. Peabody and go to bed.

Discipline at Groton was strict. The worst offense was being late; the next worst offense was being lazy. Students were expected to have lots of school spirit and to show proper respect to upper classmen.

A Strict Curriculum

The curriculum at Groton was also modeled after that of English boarding schools. It included English, mathematics, and history, and was very heavy in languages, especially Greek, Latin, French, and German. There was little science and no economics.

A special feature was "sacred studies." Dr. Peabody believed it was a Christian duty for members of the upper class to serve society. Accordingly, the school ran a summer camp for poor boys in New Hampshire, and students were expected to work there as counsellors. They were also expected to help needy people in the community.

One of those Franklin helped was an 84-year-old black woman named Mrs. Freeman, who lived alone. "We paid our first visit to her today, right after church," Franklin wrote to his parents, "and talked and gave her the latest news, for nearly an hour. We are to visit her a couple of times a week, see that she has coal, water, etc., feed her hens if they need it, and in case of a snow-storm we are to dig her out and put things ship-shape." At first Franklin signed his letters home "Nilknarf," which was his name spelled backwards. Soon, however, he was signing them "F.D.R."

An Outsider

Groton was Franklin's first experience away from his parents and the sheltered environment of his childhood. It was difficult in the beginning. He was not only homesick, he felt like an outsider.

The other boys in Franklin's class had been attending Groton since they were 12 and had already formed friendships. Franklin was the "new kid on the block." He was also a little bit different. Because he had spent so much time visiting relatives in England, he spoke with a slight British accent. And although he dressed like the other boys, his clothes were specially made by a London tailor.

The sports in which Franklin excelled, such as sailing and horseback riding, were not considered important at Groton. To be a hero there, you had to play football or baseball. Franklin was too slight to make the football varsity, and he was terrible at baseball.

Franklin's initial reaction to Groton was to cover up his feelings of being an outsider with snobbishness. He adopted a cocky attitude toward the other boys and picked frequent arguments with them. After a while, though, he decided there must be a better way. So he put his mind to becoming a "regular guy."

Some Social Successes

To prove he was not a sissy, Franklin took a few demerits in behavior. He became manager of Groton's baseball team in his senior year and acted in the senior class play. He also wrote for the school paper, learned to play the mandolin so he could entertain at parties, and sang in the choir—at least until his voice changed.

Franklin also developed into a first-rate debater. On one occasion, he argued against the annexation of Hawaii. After all, he pointed out, the United States already owned the port of Pearl Harbor. "A little inexpensive dredging" would turn it into an excellent naval base, thus making it unnecessary to take over the Hawaiian Islands as a whole. Franklin's team won the debate. However, it lost another one in which Franklin argued in favor of increasing the size of the U.S. Navy.

Franklin's efforts to become a social success paid off to some extent. By the time he graduated from Groton in 1900, he was well respected, although not particularly popular.

By this time, too, Franklin was a handsome young man. He stood a little over six feet tall, with brownish-blond hair, blue eyes, and teeth that had been straightened by wearing a dental brace for several years. Even the "specks" he now had to use—a pair of pince-nez, or glasses held on the nose by a spring—did not detract from his striking good looks.

Chapter 2
College, Marriage, and Career

Franklin entered Harvard University, in Cambridge, Massachusetts, in the fall of 1900. He would have much preferred going to the U.S. Naval Academy at Annapolis, Maryland, and becoming a naval officer. But James Roosevelt had gone to Harvard and wanted his son to do the same. So Harvard it was.

A HARVARD MAN

At Harvard, Franklin and his best friend from Groton, Lathrop "Jake" Brown, rented a corner suite of rooms in a section of Cambridge where graduates of other prep schools also lived. All the students who lived on the Gold Coast, as that area of Cambridge was known, came from rich, socially prominent families from the eastern seaboard. They ate together at special tables in the college dining halls, they contented themselves with obtaining a gentlemanly "C" average in their courses, and they had nothing to do with students who had attended public high schools.

Franklin, as usual, was a little bit different. True, all his associates were Gold Coast boys, and he did not pay much attention to his studies. However, Franklin took seriously the Roosevelt family tradition of civic responsibility, which had been reinforced by Dr. Peabody at Groton. While attending Harvard, Franklin spent several hours a week as a volunteer teacher at a settlement house in a Boston slum. He also organized a letter-writing campaign to southern colleges urging them to follow Harvard's example and admit black students.

As he had at Groton, Franklin devoted much of his time and energy trying to win popularity. As before, he was a failure at sports. He also failed to be chosen for Porcellian, the swankiest club at Harvard, an event he later called "the greatest disappointment" of his life. He did, however, make the second most exclusive club, Fly, as well as several other groups.

A Major Scoop

Franklin's chief success at Harvard was on the school's daily newspaper, *The Harvard Crimson*. He managed to get on the paper's staff in his freshman year, and worked his way up to be editor-in-chief in his senior year. In later years, he referred to his experience on the *Crimson* as "the most useful preparation I had in college for public service."

Actually, most of Franklin's editorials were rather limited in nature. They dealt with such topics as the need for fire escapes in the dormitories and "constant support" for the football team. But his activities on the *Crimson* did enable Franklin to meet and work with students who had not gone to prep school. To the dismay of his Gold Coast friends, he convinced some of the non-Gold Coast boys to run for school office. Surprisingly, however, he never ran for an office himself while at Harvard.

It was during the spring of his freshman year that Franklin scored a major scoop. Cousin Teddy—his fifth cousin Theodore Roosevelt, who was then Vice-President of the United States—had come to Cambridge to visit a friend, Professor Abbott Lowell. Franklin telephoned his cousin and learned that the Vice-President was lecturing to Professor Lowell's class in government the next day. Franklin then rushed to his office at the *Crimson* and wrote up the story for the paper's front page. As a result, almost the entire student body tried to crowd into Professor Lowell's classroom to hear the Vice-President.

A NEW INFLUENCE

Theodore Roosevelt was fast becoming an important influence on Franklin—especially since the death of James Roosevelt in the winter of 1900. Like Franklin himself, Cousin Teddy was a little bit different.

Most Roosevelts looked down on party politics. As Sara Roosevelt put it, "There is something vulgar about fighting in the political arena." Theodore Roosevelt had been in party politics for years. Among other things, he had been a member of the New York state legislature, assistant secretary of the navy, and governor of New York before being elected Vice-President.

Then, in September 1901, President William McKinley was assassinated, and Cousin Teddy was elevated to the presidency. Always ready to fight for what he considered right, Theodore Roosevelt launched a program he called the Square Deal. It was based on the idea that the federal government was responsible for the national welfare. President Roosevelt claimed that rugged individualism worked well in a simple, poor, agricultural society, but it did not work as well in a complex, rich, industrial society, such as the United States had become. If the nation were to develop in an orderly manner, President Roosevelt believed, the federal government had to step in to prevent economic abuses.

Accordingly, Theodore Roosevelt started a series of attacks against the trusts, or large business combines, that were running the American economy. His actions horrified Harvard's Gold Coast students, who called him "a traitor to his class." That may have been one reason Franklin did not make Porcellian.

Franklin, however, was enthusiastic about his cousin's program. Franklin believed it was absolutely right to champion the cause of the underdog. So he became active in the Harvard Political Club, made several trips to Washington, and in 1904 cast his first presidential vote for Theodore Roosevelt, even though he was a Democrat and the President was not.

FRANKLIN AND ELEANOR

It was also in 1904 that Franklin made an announcement that greatly displeased Sara Roosevelt. He became engaged to Anna Eleanor Roosevelt, the President's favorite niece and Franklin's fifth cousin once removed.

Cousin Eleanor

Ever since the death of James Roosevelt, his widow had become more attached than ever to her only child. She had even moved from Hyde Park to Cambridge to be near him while he was attending Harvard. And she was looking forward to having him return with her to Hyde Park after graduation to take up the life of a country gentleman. The idea that Franklin wanted to get married at the age of 22 was a great shock.

What is more, Sara did not consider Eleanor the best choice for her handsome and charming son. Oh, Eleanor was acceptable. Her family was certainly of the right kind, and she had an adequate income from her late parents' estates. She had traveled extensively in Europe and spoke several languages. But she was almost six feet tall and quite gawky, her front teeth protruded, and she was much too shy and serious to be a social success. Why, she spent most of her time teaching working-class people at a New York City settlement house!

To Franklin, however, Eleanor's strong social conscience was very attractive. He found her intelligent, sweet-tempered, honest, and sensitive. And he liked her enormous blue eyes and the smile that made her face light up.

For her part, Eleanor had had a crush on her cousin ever since she was 15. The two of them had attended a Christmas party given by another cousin. Franklin had been dancing with all the popular girls when he noticed Eleanor standing by herself against the wall, dressed in a child's short skirt instead of a ballgown, and looking as if she were about to cry. Perhaps because he himself knew what it felt like to be left out, Franklin had asked Eleanor for the next dance.

A Last-Ditch Fight

Like other parents who disapprove of a child's proposed marriage, Sara Roosevelt tried to break it up. First, she refused to formally announce the engagement. Franklin responded by writing, "I know my mind. And as for you, dear Mummy, you know that nothing can ever change what we have always been and always will be to each other." Eleanor, too, tried to reassure Sara. "I know just how you feel and how hard it must be, but I do so want you to learn to love me a little. You must know that I will always try to do what you wish."

Sara then suggested that Franklin and roommate Lathrop Brown accompany her on a Caribbean cruise for six weeks to "think things over." Franklin agreed, and had a grand time visiting Cuba, Curaçao, Puerto Rico, and Trinidad. But despite a shipboard flirtation with a French girl, he returned to Boston as determined as ever to marry Eleanor.

Next, Mrs. Roosevelt took Franklin to Washington to see if she could obtain a job for him as a secretary in the U.S. embassy in London. But he was considered too young for such a position.

At last, Sara Roosevelt resigned herself to the idea that Franklin and Eleanor were going to get married. The wedding date was set for the spring of 1905, when Franklin would be in his first year of law school at Columbia University.

An Unusual Wedding

Franklin and Eleanor's wedding took place on March 17. The young couple chose St. Patrick's Day because President Theodore Roosevelt, who was going to give the bride away, was coming to New York to review the St. Patrick's Day parade. The event turned out to be quite different from the usual society wedding.

For one thing, the site of the ceremony—the house of yet another cousin—was located just around the corner from Fifth Avenue, where the parade took place. There was so much noise from the brass bands playing Irish songs that it was almost impossible to hear the wedding march.

In addition, President Roosevelt was followed to the house not only by the usual escort of police and Secret Service men but also by a crowd of people chanting "We want Teddy! We want Teddy!" The mob grew so large that some of the invited guests could not get in. Even Franklin had to push and shove his way through the door.

The wedding itself was beautiful. Eleanor looked radiant in a heavy white satin gown, a collar of pearls, and her grandmother's veil of Brussels lace. Lathrop Brown was best man, President Roosevelt's daughter Alice was maid of honor, and the ceremony was performed by Dr. Peabody. When the ceremony was over, the President congratulated his niece on keeping the Roosevelt name in the family and went into the library for refreshments. The guests all crowded after him — and the bride and groom found themselves left alone in the parlor. Eleanor was hurt, but Franklin just laughed and suggested that they follow the crowd.

The End of the Honeymoon

The young couple moved into an apartment hotel following their marriage, and Franklin resumed his legal studies at Columbia. That summer, when the university was closed, they took a three-month tour of Europe. Franklin bought naval prints to add to his collection; Eleanor bought yards of beautiful red damask to use for upholstery. And in Scotland, they bought the first in what was to be a long succession of Scottish terriers.

When they returned to New York, Franklin and Eleanor moved into a house in mid-Manhattan that Sara Roosevelt had rented, staffed, and furnished for "her children." Franklin was delighted with his mother's thoughtfulness and generosity. Eleanor, however, was crushed that she did not have a chance to pick out her own furnishings. But she knew nothing about running a house, and she wanted very much to please her mother-in-law.

The move set a pattern for the young couple's marriage. A few years later, Sara Roosevelt built two adjoining houses on East 68th Street in Manhattan, one for herself and the other for her son and his family. Sliding doors between the two living rooms made communication easy. And, as before, the furnishings were chosen by Sara.

The Roosevelts' first child, Anna, was born in 1906. She

Franklin and Eleanor Roosevelt with their five children and Franklin's mother, Sara (at right), in 1919. (Franklin D. Roosevelt Library.)

was followed by five more children over the next 10 years: James (1907); the first Franklin, Jr. (1909), who died in infancy of influenza; Elliott (1910); the second Franklin, Jr. (1914); and John (1916). In this area, too, Sara Roosevelt took over. She hired the children's English nursemaids, bought the children's clothes, and loaded them with presents. Except for an occasional outburst of frustrated tears, Eleanor went along.

She also went along with her husband's outgoing, fun-loving nature. Franklin enjoyed attending parties, playing stud poker at the University Club, and sailing, riding, and golfing during the summer at Campobello. Eleanor seldom shared her husband's activities; she simply wanted him to be happy.

A YOUNG ATTORNEY

After completing his law studies at Columbia, Franklin passed the New York State bar examination in 1907 and was hired as a clerk by one of New York City's most highly respected law firms. Although he received no pay his first year, the income from his and Eleanor's inheritances, combined with frequent checks from his mother, allowed the young Roosevelts to live very well.

Over the next two years, Franklin handled a number of important cases, including one in which he defended a major company in an antitrust suit. But he was really not interested in contracts, deeds, wills, and other legal documents. He had become a lawyer only because it was considered an appropriate occupation for a well-to-do man.

Franklin also tried some business ventures, but without much success. He made several excellent suggestions for modernizing the farm at Hyde Park, only to be told by Sara Roosevelt that she intended to keep on running it just the way James had run it. Franklin did, however, buy up some abandoned farms in the area and plant them with evergreens from the state forestry service to restore the soil.

By 1910, it was clear to Franklin that he was bored stiff. There must be *something* interesting and worthwhile that he could do.

Chapter 3
Political Beginnings

When Franklin was five years old, his father was offered a diplomatic post abroad by President Grover Cleveland. When James Roosevelt went to Washington to decline the offer, he took his son along with him. As President Cleveland solemnly shook hands with his young visitor, he told Franklin, "My little man, I am making a strange wish for you. I hope that you may never be President of the United States."

Franklin looked up at the rotund and amiable Cleveland and replied, "But *you* don't look unhappy, Mr. President."

Whereupon President Cleveland turned to James Roosevelt and observed, "Your son, I see, has at least one quality for a successful politician. A clever tongue."

THE FIRST CAMPAIGN

In the spring of 1910, when he was 28 years old, Franklin was asked by the Democratic leaders of Columbia, Putnam, and Dutchess counties in New York to run for the state senate. He was a good choice from their point of view. The Roosevelt name was well-known in the area, and Franklin had enough money to pay his own expenses and even contribute to the party's general campaign fund. In a way, however, it was a thankless offer. The district had been overwhelmingly Republican for years. In fact, no Democratic state senator had been elected from the district since 1856.

Franklin, however, was delighted. At last he had a chance to try something really different! Furthermore, Theodore Roosevelt had started *his* political career as a senator in the New York state legislature – and Franklin still hero-worshiped his cousin. Sara Roosevelt, however, sniffed disapprovingly. Why on earth did Franklin want to get involved in such a "messy business"? Eleanor, as usual, went along, even though at the time she was not interested in politics and did not even think that women should have the right to vote.

Franklin threw himself energetically into his campaign, running with great flair and imagination. Instead of using a horse and buggy, he rented a bright-red Maxwell touring car that had no windshield or top. As one of the few automobiles in the area, it attracted a tremendous amount of attention. It also enabled the young candidate to visit every town and village in the district. The one community Franklin did not bother about was the Democratic town of Poughkeepsie. He realized that the only way he could win was by spending all his time working to gain the support of Republican farmers.

Franklin talked to the farmers about the need for a standard-size apple barrel so there would be no disagreements over how many apples were bought and sold. He discussed the importance of planting trees and other methods of conserving soil. He was careful to have his driver stop the Maxwell whenever they met a farmer riding a horse so as not to frighten the animal with the car's roaring, clanking noise.

Although Franklin spoke with an upper-class accent and was not yet the great orator he later became, his speeches struck a responsive chord with his listeners. They liked the young candidate's honesty, his knowledge of farm problems, and his obvious determination. They also liked his jovial spirit and personal charm. Moreover, they were flattered that he had taken the trouble to campaign directly for their vote. No previous candidate had ever paid them much attention.

When the ballots for state senator were counted, Franklin—to everyone's surprise—was the winner by a comfortable margin of more than 1,100 votes.

STATE SENATOR

In those years, the New York state legislature usually sat for only three months. As a result, most legislators lived in boardinghouses in the state capital of Albany and went home on weekends. Franklin, in contrast, rented a three-story, furnished house and moved his wife and children to the capital.

Fighting Tammany Hall

Franklin was determined not to get lost in the crowd at Albany. An opportunity to move into the political limelight opened up almost at once.

Before 1913, United States senators were elected by state legislatures rather than by popular vote. Because the Democratic Party was in control of the state legislature in Albany, the next U.S. senator from New York obviously would be a Democrat. Tammany Hall, the Democratic Party organization in New York City, was backing William F. "Blue-eyed Billy" Sheehan for the job. However, other Democratic legislators did not like "Blue-eyed Billy." They thought even less of big-city political machines like Tammany Hall.

Many of the newspaper correspondents in Albany did not like Sheehan or Tammany Hall either. Among them was a long-time political reporter from Indiana named Louis McHenry Howe. Howe was "an ugly little man" with rumpled clothes who chain-smoked cigarettes and was always dropping ashes on his vest. He had been put off at first by Franklin's upper-class accent and by the fact that Franklin wore a top hat, morning coat, and striped trousers on formal occasions. He referred to the freshman state senator as "a spoiled, silk pants sort of guy."

However, Howe soon realized that Franklin showed great promise as a political leader. He even had the makings of a statesman. Howe liked Franklin's ideas about the evils of bossism. "Public office means serving the public and nobody else," Franklin often said.

When Franklin decided to support Sheehan's opponent, Edward M. Shepard, for the U.S. Senate, Howe helped him work out a simple but effective strategy. Franklin lined up 21 fellow Democratic rebels. Every day at noon, they would report for the legislative roll call. As soon as it was over, they would walk out. This left the Democrats without enough votes to elect "Blue-eyed Billy." The rebels would then adjourn to the Roosevelt house for the afternoon and evening. There, they would smoke cigars and talk politics until Eleanor brought in sandwiches and coffee.

The stalemate between Roosevelt's rebels and Tammany Hall continued for three months. Finally, the two sides agreed to a compromise. Both Sheehan and Shepard withdrew, and a third candidate was elected U.S. senator.

As a result of his efforts, Franklin became known all over the state of New York as a fighter for better government. Even politicians in Washington became familiar with his name. Tammany Hall members, though, were disgusted. "This puppy is still young," one of them snorted. "Wouldn't it be better to drown him before he grows up?"

A Social Reformer

Despite opposition from Tammany Hall, Franklin was appointed chairman of the state senate's Forest, Fish and Game Commission. He promptly began waging a fight to save the forests of the Hudson River Valley, where lumber firms were cutting down all the trees, section by section, without replanting. Franklin pointed out that without trees, the fertile valley would soon turn into a wasteland. It was the trees that held the soil in place, enriched it with fallen leaves, and caused clouds to drop their moisture. Without trees, New York's farmland would erode and its economy would suffer. Franklin's arguments were so convincing that the state legislature passed a law requiring logging companies to harvest only selected trees and to plant tree seedlings as replacements.

Franklin championed many other reforms. He advocated purer milk at lower prices for poor children, and free medical service for the needy. He pushed for the development of electric power. He favored the right of women to vote and the popular election of U.S. senators. He urged that the work week for boys between the ages of 16 and 21 be limited to 54 hours. In short, he tried to help the weak against the strong and to broaden the people's role in government. It was a course he would follow throughout his career.

Running for Re-election

In 1912, Franklin ran again for the state senate. This time, however, he did not make a single speech or even a single public appearance. An attack of typhoid fever struck the Roosevelt family in August. Eleanor made a quick recovery, but Franklin became so seriously ill that he was confined to bed.

Nevertheless, Franklin mounted an aggressive campaign. Louis Howe flooded Columbia, Putnam, and Dutchess counties with Franklin's name. Letters were sent to every voter, with even Sara and Eleanor helping to mail them out. Posters in store fronts proclaimed Franklin as "Needed in the Fight for Conservation" and "Labor's Best Friend in Albany." And newspaper advertisements reminded people that "When Franklin Roosevelt says he will fight for a thing, it means he won't quit until he wins."

The technique worked. Franklin was re-elected, this time

by a margin of 1,700 votes. From then on, Howe was F.D.R.'s closest political advisor.

ASSISTANT SECRETARY OF THE NAVY

Although Franklin was returned to Albany, many other Democrats were not, and the Republicans regained control of the state legislature. Democrats fared better nationally, however, as they captured both Congress and the White House.

In March 1913, Franklin went to Washington to witness the inauguration of Woodrow Wilson as 28th President of the United States. Franklin had supported Wilson for the nomination, organizing Democrats-for-Wilson clubs throughout upper New York state despite the opposition of Tammany Hall. Perhaps, he thought, he might be offered a position in the new administration.

As luck would have it, he was. Josephus Daniels, a newspaper editor from North Carolina, had met Franklin at the Democratic National Convention in 1912 and had been greatly impressed by his vigor and grasp of politics. Daniels was Wilson's choice for secretary of the navy. Would Franklin be interested in the post of assistant secretary?

Franklin was overjoyed. What could be better? Hadn't he loved ships and the sea ever since he was a young boy? Hadn't he wanted to become a naval officer when he grew up? Didn't he own almost 10,000 pamphlets about the U.S. Navy, of which he had read all but one? And once again, he would be following in his Cousin Teddy's footsteps.

"How would I like it?" Franklin said to Daniels. "I'd like it bully well."

The appointment was confirmed by the U.S. Senate, making Franklin, at the age of 31, the youngest man ever to hold the post of assistant secretary of the navy. He, Eleanor, and the children moved to Washington, D.C., into the house that Theodore Roosevelt had occupied before becoming President. Howe and his family also moved to Washington because Franklin wanted Howe to be his executive assistant.

Strengthening the Navy

Franklin dove into his job as assistant secretary by carrying out a survey of the U.S. Navy. To his dismay, he found it in very poor condition. "We are supposed to have 36 or 37 battleships built or building," he reported. "We have 16." And many of the 16 could not even go to sea for lack of crews. Franklin promptly mounted an energetic campaign for more ships and more men.

He also worked hard to improve the navy's efficiency. He visited every government shipyard in the country to determine whether it should be improved or abandoned. To eliminate graft, he changed the methods for purchasing supplies. He promoted officers on the basis of merit instead of length of service, and he insisted that every sailor learn how to swim. When Howe pointed out that workers at the shipyards were receiving extremely low wages, Franklin set up a system of collective bargaining. As sailors say, he ran a tight ship.

A Valuable Lesson

Franklin was very happy in Washington. Unlike football, baseball, and the law, politics was an activity that he loved. Furthermore, it was one in which he excelled. He couldn't wait to move ahead. So in the summer of 1914, he declared himself a candidate for the Democratic nomination for U.S. senator from New York.

To Franklin's embarrassment, he was overwhelmed in the primary by the Tammany Hall candidate, James W. Gerard. However, as Franklin later admitted, he had only himself to blame. Howe, who had not been consulted beforehand, disapproved of his running. Franklin had also underestimated the resourcefulness of Tammany Hall, which put up a highly respected candidate. In short, he had simply been too cocky.

It was a valuable lesson. From then on, Franklin paid a great deal of attention to improving his ties with different factions of the Democratic Party. He also became more patient, at least as far as his personal ambitions were concerned.

World War I

When World War I broke out in Europe in 1914, Franklin held that "a war in any one continent is a direct threat to the peace of all other continents." His view, however, did not have wide acceptance. President Wilson promptly announced that the United States would maintain its traditional policy of not becoming involved in European affairs. The United States, he declared, would not support either the Allied Powers — which included Great Britain, France, and Russia — or the Central Powers — which included Germany and Austria-Hungary. The vast majority of the American people agreed with Wilson.

Franklin, on the other hand, was certain the United States could not remain neutral indefinitely. To him, the Atlantic Ocean, rather than protecting America, was a highway that could be used by merchant ships and aggressors alike.

Within 2½ years, Franklin was proven right. Beginning in 1915, Germany waged unrestricted submarine warfare in the Atlantic. It sank unarmed passenger liners and merchant ships as well as warships. Hundreds of Americans lost their lives. Finally, in April 1917, the United States entered World War I on the side of the Allies.

Over the next 1½ years, Assistant Secretary of the Navy Franklin Roosevelt worked harder than he had ever done in his life. He pushed and prodded and cut corners everywhere. "My way to handle long consultations about things that have to be done is to grab a pair of scissors and to slash away at the red tape," he said.

For example, on June 27, 1917, Franklin examined a site

where quarters for navy personnel were to be built. The next day, he gave the contractor the go-ahead for the job. Ground was broken on July 5, and on the morning of August 11, 6,800 sailors sat down to breakfast in their new mess hall. In October, Franklin received official permission to have the quarters built!

In addition to strengthening the navy, Franklin kept an open mind to new ideas. One idea that was brought to his attention was for installing a curtain of electric mines under the North Sea to protect Allied shipping against attacks by German submarines. American admirals scoffed at the idea, but Franklin convinced the British Navy that it was a good one. The North Sea Mine Barrage eventually destroyed more than 200 German submarines.

Despite his accomplishments, Franklin wanted to get out from behind his desk and join the navy. But when he asked Wilson to release him from his post, the President refused. "You are too valuable to us just where you are," Wilson told Franklin.

Finally, in the summer of 1918, the President agreed to send Franklin to Europe to inspect American naval stations there. While in France, he took the opportunity to visit the battlefields, where he saw the horror of war at first hand. He also narrowly escaped having his car blown up by a German shell.

On the way home, Franklin became ill with double pneumonia. By the time he recovered, the Allies had won and the war was over. Franklin returned to Europe to supervise the dismantling of American naval installations and the sale of surplus government property. He then repeated the job in the United States. By August 1920, his work was finished. He resigned as assistant secretary of the navy—to once again follow in his Cousin Teddy's footsteps. At the 1920 Democratic National Convention, Franklin was chosen to run for Vice-President of the United States.

FRANKLIN AND LUCY

In the meantime, a major change had taken place in Franklin's personal life. Soon after the Roosevelts moved to Washington in 1913, Eleanor hired a social secretary named Lucy Page Mercer to schedule appointments and help answer all the mail that the wife of a high government official received. Lucy was just 22 at the time, and very pretty. Franklin always referred to her as "the lovely Lucy." She was also extremely competent, and Eleanor was pleased to have her.

This was especially so after the United States entered World War I. In common with other Washington wives, Eleanor became very active in volunteer work. She helped organize the Navy Red Cross, served in Red Cross canteens, and ran the knitting program at the Navy Department. She liked the work immensely; she had always been interested in social service. In addition, it gave her a sense of worth and self-reliance. Franklin worked very long hours, and even when he was home, Louis Howe always seemed to be there, too. The children paid more attention to grandmother Sara than to her. And she and Franklin had never developed a really close, sharing relationship.

When Franklin returned from Europe in 1918 with double pneumonia, he was ordered to bed at once, so Eleanor unpacked his luggage. As she did so, she found some love letters from Lucy Mercer. A family conference was held. Franklin stated that he loved Lucy and wanted to marry her. Sara threatened to disown her son if he got a divorce. Eleanor said she would agree to a divorce only if it would not hurt the children too much.

In the end, Franklin decided to stay married to Eleanor. It may have been his strong feelings for "the chicks," as he called his children. It may have been the threatened loss of his inheritance, or perhaps the effect of a divorce on his political career. It may have been the fact that Lucy was Roman

Catholic and therefore unlikely to marry a divorced man. In any event, Franklin promised not to see her again.

The Roosevelt marriage, however, was never the same after that. As Eleanor said in later years, "I can forgive, but I cannot forget." From then on, she threw herself into all kinds of public service, such as establishing programs for the needy and writing a daily newspaper column. She also did everything she could to help her husband in his political career. But while there was mutual respect and admiration between Franklin and Eleanor, there was no longer any love.

THE 1920 CAMPAIGN

Even before the Democratic and Republican national conventions met, it was clear that 1920 would be a Republican year. President Wilson had suffered two paralyzing strokes. He had also failed in his attempts to persuade the Senate to support the League of Nations. Following the end of World War I, Wilson believed that only an international organization could maintain peace in the world. Franklin agreed. But most Americans were sick and tired of Europe and its problems. They were also frightened by a wave of labor strikes and worried lest communism develop in the United States the way it had in Russia. So, as is usual in such a situation, the people were ready to take out their frustrations on the political party in power.

Under the circumstances, the Democrats had a hard time finding anyone willing to run for President. After 44 ballots, they finally settled on a comparative unknown, former Governor of Ohio James M. Cox. Then—to Franklin Roosevelt's surprise—he was nominated for Vice-President.

Actually, it was a smart choice. Franklin had done an excellent job as assistant secretary of the navy during the war. He bore the Roosevelt name, and once he was offered the opportunity, he was eager to run.

As he had in previous political races, Franklin ran for the vice-presidency in 1920 with energy and enthusiasm. His tall, hand-some figure added to his appeal on the campaign trail. (Globe Photos.)

Franklin threw himself into the campaign with his usual vigor and good cheer. Traveling by train and automobile, he delivered more than 1,000 speeches in 42 states, averaging seven a day. With increasing eloquence, he argued for such progressive policies as soil conservation and labor reform, as well as for the League of Nations. Over and over, he asserted his belief that a revitalized federal government could help meet people's needs. "We can never go back. The 'good old days' are gone past forever; we have no regrets. . . . We must go forward or flounder."

Although, as expected, the ticket of Cox and Roosevelt was soundly defeated by Republicans Warren G. Harding and Calvin Coolidge, the campaign was nevertheless a big plus for Franklin. He saw all parts of the country "as only a candidate for national office or a traveling salesman can" and impressed local party leaders with his ability and charm. He developed a close working relationship with several aides who would later serve him in the White House, notably Marguerite "Missy" LeHand. And Eleanor, for the first time, grew to like and trust Louis Howe. In fact, Howe often went over Franklin's speeches with her because she made so many useful suggestions.

Neither Franklin nor Howe was discouraged by the Republican landslide. As Franklin put it, "The moment of defeat is the best time to lay plans for a future victory." As for Howe, he had been addressing his chief in letters and memos as "Most Revered Future President" since 1912. He had also developed the practice of sending out personal, chatty letters over Roosevelt's signature to every state, county, and city Democratic politician Franklin met. Both men were confident that despite the 1920 election, it was only a matter of time before Franklin made a run for the presidency.

Then, in the summer of 1921, disaster struck.

Chapter 4

A Turning Point

Following the defeat of the Cox-Roosevelt ticket in November 1920, Franklin spent the first few months of 1921 putting his personal affairs in order. He took a job as vice-president of an insurance company, formed a small law partnership, and invested in several business ventures. In line with the family tradition, he also served as president of the Navy Club, chairman of the Boy Scouts of New York, and an overseer of Harvard. In addition, he helped organize the Woodrow Wilson Foundation, which sponsors students of international affairs.

By the time summer rolled round, Franklin was tired. So, for the first time since the end of the war, he decided to join his family at Campobello for a vacation.

A VACATION THAT CHANGED HISTORY

With his characteristic enthusiasm, Franklin threw himself into vacation activities — sailing, fishing, and swimming in the Bay of Fundy. One day, as the family was returning from a sail, they spotted a brush fire on a nearby island. They immediately beached the boat and beat out the flames with tree boughs. Hot, tired, and smeared with ashes, they went for a swim in a lake on Campobello and then ran about two miles back to the house. Because Franklin still did not feel invigorated, he took a plunge into the bay. He said later that he "never felt anything so cold as that water." When he returned to the house, he found a pile of mail waiting for him. Without changing out of his wet bathing suit, he sat down on the porch and spent several hours going through his correspondence.

When Franklin woke the next morning, he had a fever and pains in his back and legs. The doctor who was called in thought it was "just a bad cold." Two days later, Franklin found himself unable to walk or even to hold a pen in his hand. The specialist who was sent for said the problem was a blood clot in the lower spinal column, and recommended daily massage. For two weeks, Eleanor and Howe took turns rubbing Franklin's back and legs. Howe also read Franklin's mail aloud to him and wrote out his answers. But the fever and the pains persisted.

Finally, another specialist was called in. This time, the diagnosis was poliomyelitis, or infantile paralysis, commonly known as polio. The prognosis was that Franklin would be crippled for life. He would never be able to walk, stand, or sit down by himself, nor would he be able to dress or undress without help. Asleep or awake, he could never be left alone.

A CRUCIAL DECISION

At that point, Franklin had a choice. He could follow the wishes of his mother, Sara, who urged him to forget about business and politics, retire to Hyde Park, and live comfortably as a permanent invalid. Or he could follow the advice of Eleanor and Howe, who wanted him to return to his usual activities as soon as he could. Howe, in fact, would not even consider the possibility that F.D.R.'s political career was over. "By gad, legs or no legs, Franklin will be President," he said.

Eleanor and Howe won. Or rather, Franklin did. He kept

his fears about the future to himself and turned a cheerful face to those around him. Month after month, he struggled to "[conquer the flesh] by will and spirit." He spent long hours pulling himself up on gymnasts' rings above his bed to strengthen his chest, neck, and arm muscles. After a while he was able to sit up in a wheel chair. Next, he took to crawling from room to room on his hands and knees. Then he began dragging himself up the stairs in his house, step by step, keeping up a steady conversation as he went. Finally, he was fitted with 40-pound steel braces that enabled him to stand and even walk a little on crutches.

Throughout Franklin's ordeal, Eleanor was always there, encouraging his efforts and rejecting Sara's repeated assertions that he was over-exerting himself. Howe, who moved into the Roosevelt house to help, often quoted the following encouraging poem to Franklin:

> In the full clutch of circumstance,
> I have not winced, nor cried out loud,
> And under the bludgeonings of chance
> My head is bloody but unbowed.
>
> It matters not how strait the gate,
> How charged with punishment the scroll,
> I am the master of my fate,
> I am the captain of my soul.

As Franklin struggled to overcome his physical disability, his personality underwent a change. His determination increased, and at the same time, he grew more patient. He also became less concerned with appearances and more understanding of others. In the past, his attitude toward needy people had been a bit patronizing. Now, he realized what needing help really meant. As Howe put it, Franklin "began to see the other fellow's point of view. He thought of others who were ill and afflicted and in want. He dwelt on many things that had not bothered him much before. Lying there, he grew bigger, day by day."

Before long, Franklin was looking at the bright side of things and even joking about his condition. "Maybe my legs aren't so good, but look at those shoulders. Jack Dempsey [the world's heavyweight boxing champion] would be green with envy." F.D.R. also came to believe that nothing was impossible. "If you have spent two years in bed trying to wiggle your big toe, everything else seems easy."

BACK IN POLITICS

As Franklin's energy returned, he began going down to his office, first one day, then two days, and finally four days a week. He carried on his insurance business in the mornings and his legal work in the afternoons. He formed a new law partnership, tried some new business ventures, and became head of the American Construction Council, an attempt by the building industry to set standards for itself.

More importantly, Franklin renewed his interest in politics. He lent his name to several Democratic fund-raising campaigns, and he and Howe kept in touch by letter with Democratic Party members all over the country. Whenever there was a Democratic meeting, there was a message from F.D.R. Sometimes it was about the need for a new international organization to replace the League of Nations. Sometimes it was a stirring call to free the government from the "professional moneymakers" of the Republican Party. And sometimes it was simply congratulations on an election victory.

In politics, too, Eleanor proved a great asset. Because it was difficult for Franklin to attend political meetings, Eleanor did it for him. She found public speaking hard at first. Her voice often turned shrill, and she would giggle at the oddest moments. But Howe would sit in the back row and criticize her speech on the way home, and after a while Eleanor became a first-rate public speaker. She was always inviting the politicians she met to come to New York City or to Hyde Park to talk with Franklin. And come they did.

THE 1924 CONVENTION

In 1924, F.D.R. made his first public appearance since becoming paralyzed. It took place at the Democratic National Convention in New York City. Franklin was not a candidate, but he was scheduled to deliver the nominating speech for Governor Alfred E. Smith of New York. Smith was one of the two leading contenders for the presidential nomination and the first Roman Catholic to be seriously considered for that office.

When the time came for F.D.R. to speak, he rose from his wheelchair and, with the help of his son James, made his way slowly to the speaker's stand. As the audience cheered, Franklin flashed a big smile and tossed his head back with an upward tilt of his chin. Then he handed his crutches to his son, took a firm hold on the edge of the stand to balance himself, and began to speak.

For more than 30 minutes, F.D.R. criticized the corruption and scandals of the Republican administration. He praised Smith's progressive record as governor—his ability to strike at error and eradicate wrong-doing. As to Smith's personal qualifications, Franklin stated: "He has a personality that carries to every hearer not only the sincerity but the righteousness of what he says. He is the 'Happy Warrior' of the political battlefield."

The resulting ovation lasted for over an hour. It was not so much for Smith's nomination as it was for F.D.R. himself. To most of the people present, it was Roosevelt who was the real "Happy Warrior." As the *New York World* said in an editorial: "Franklin D. Roosevelt stands out as the real hero of the Democratic Convention of 1924. Adversity has lifted him above the bickering, the religious bigotry, conflicting personal ambitions and petty sectional prejudices. It has made him the one leader commanding the respect and admiration of delegations from all sections of the land."

Despite Franklin's magnificent speech, Smith lost the nomination to John W. Davis. The Democrats also lost the fall election to the Republican ticket of Calvin Coolidge and Charles G. Dawes. But F.D.R. had taken a giant step on the road to the White House.

INTERLUDE AT WARM SPRINGS

During 1924 Franklin started a new kind of physical therapy. A friend of his named George Peabody owned an inn in Warm Springs, Georgia, about 75 miles south of Atlanta. Near the inn was a natural pool of mineral water with a temperature of 88 degrees. The Creek Indians who had once lived in the area believed the spring had healing powers, so they used to bring their sick and their wounded warriors there. More recently, Peabody informed Franklin, a man named Louis Joseph, also afflicted with polio, had recovered the use of his arms and legs by swimming and exercising in the pool. Why didn't Franklin try it?

Franklin did just that. Because the water was so heavy with mineral salts, he found he could stay in it for several hours a day without becoming tired. He swam, he did underwater exercises, he played ball with Louis Howe and other swimmers. Soon he was able to stand upright without his braces and even take a few steps without his crutches — but only so long as he remained in the pool.

Franklin's presence at Warm Springs was big news in the area. The local newspapers sent reporters, and one of them wrote an article called "Swimming Back to Health" that was reprinted in papers throughout the country. Soon other polio victims began arriving at Warm Springs, many without money. The inn's owner wanted to send them home, but Franklin would not hear of it.

At his own expense, F.D.R. built a second pool and a separate dining room for the polio victims to use so the resort's regular guests would not become alarmed. He saw to it that "his gang" was housed and fed. He taught the new "patients" how to swim and do underwater exercises. Most importantly, "Doc" Roosevelt taught them to fight self-pity and to have confidence in what they could do. "It is so good to be alive even though we are a little bit sick," he told the others.

Franklin eventually bought Warm Springs and several thousand acres of surrounding land, and turned the facilities into a nonprofit rehabilitation center for polio victims. The donations and loans that he made to the center cost him about two-thirds of his fortune. When he was elected President, his private cottage at Warm Springs became "The Little White House." In 1945, it was where Franklin Delano Roosevelt died.

RE-ENTERING THE POLITICAL ARENA

Franklin did not want to run for public office again until he recovered the use of his legs. However, the 1924 presidential election had split the Democratic Party. On one side were conservative southerners who supported the 18th Amendment to the U.S. Constitution prohibiting the manufacture or sale of alcoholic beverages. They also believed that Catholics should not be party leaders or candidates for office. (In those years, many Americans believed that Catholics took direct orders from the Pope on everything and did not really understand the meaning of democracy.) On the other side were liberal northerners, mostly from industrial areas, who wanted to repeal prohibition. They also had nothing against Catholics

Prohibition

Ever since colonial days, Americans had been a drinking people. Almost everyone drank—women, children, even members of the clergy. People drank to seal a bargain, to celebrate the building of a barn, or to warm themselves before going to bed in an unheated room. People also drank to disguise the taste of the salted meat and fish that formed a large part of the American diet. And doctors gave whiskey or brandy to patients as an anesthetic before performing operations.

Then, too, politicians would give voters free drinks before an election. Grocers would treat their customers to liquor when they came into the store to pay their bill. And wages would usually include a daily allowance of whiskey, rum, or beer.

By the 1800s, people began to realize that drunkenness was a serious problem. It often led to crime, child abuse, and the like. So in 1826 they organized the first temperance society, aimed at convincing people not to use liquor. By 1857, 13 states had passed laws prohibiting the manufacture and sale of alcoholic beverages.

After the Civil War, several church-affiliated organizations—notably the Anti-Saloon League and the Women's Christian Temperance Union—took the lead in calling for nationwide prohibition. In 1920 they won their fight when the 18th Amendment to the Constitution was adopted. This amendment prohibited the manufacture and sale of alcoholic beverages in the United States.

Drinking went down, but bootlegging went up. A bootlegger was a person who smuggled illegal alcoholic beverages into the United States from Canada or some other country. The bootlegging business was run by hoodlums, who bribed judges and the police. The result was that many people lost respect for the law.

As organized crime increased and taxes to pay for enforcing prohibition went up, many Americans began to believe that prohibition was a mistake. So they started a campaign to repeal the 18th Amendment. There was a great deal of opposition to this movement, especially from rural people and from religious fundamentalists, who considered drinking a sin. Nevertheless, by the end of F.D.R.'s first year as President, the 18th Amendment was repealed by the 21st Amendment.

because many of them were Catholic themselves. Furthermore, the party was deeply in debt. The only apparent source of money was rich business people who would naturally expect favors if the Democrats won the next presidential election.

Rebuilding the Party

Franklin wanted the Democratic Party to "stand for something." He wanted it to be a progressive party that would pay attention to the needs of ordinary people, oppose religious bigotry, and take an interest in international affairs. So he and Howe went to work to pull the Democrats together again.

The two men began by writing a letter to every important Democrat in the country. The letter asked each official to describe the shape of the party in his area and to suggest ways of making things better. F.D.R. and Howe would read the replies and then add a few ideas of their own. Some were good, some were not, but the result was that Democratic leaders all over the country began taking steps to revitalize their party from the ground up. They also developed a high personal regard for F.D.R. He certainly "seemed to be a live wire" who was interested in local problems.

The 1928 Convention

As the 1928 election drew near, several people suggested to F.D.R. that he run for the presidential nomination. Franklin and Howe, however, thought it would be smarter to wait until 1932; 1928 did not look like a Democratic year. The postwar economic recession was over, the stock market was booming, and the Republicans were claiming credit for the country's prosperity. They had also chosen a highly respected and very popular person as their presidential candidate—Herbert Hoover.

So, as he had done four years earlier, Franklin went to the Democratic National Convention and nominated Alfred E. Smith. This time, however, there were several differences. For one thing, Roosevelt's physical condition had improved so much that he was now able to walk with just one cane and the support of someone's strong arm. For another, the new medium of radio was coming into use, and the convention was broadcast by two networks, NBC and CBS. Franklin realized that radio called for a new speaking technique, and he composed his nominating speech accordingly. When he came on the air, his deep, strong voice and beautiful pronunciation made it seem as if he were sitting in his listeners' living rooms, talking directly to them as friends.

A POLITICAL DRAFT

Smith won the presidential nomination on the first ballot, and Franklin returned to Warm Springs to continue his physical therapy. But things did not go well with the Democratic campaign. Smith was a big-city man who had no understanding of farm problems and little knowledge of the country outside the eastern seaboard. His brown derbies and fancy shirts did not appeal to most people in the Middle and Far West, while the fact that he was Roman Catholic made him suspect in the South. By September, Democratic Party leaders were worried that Smith would not even be able to carry his home state of New York.

What to do? The only reasonable solution was to run a strong candidate for governor of New York, preferably one who was popular outside of New York City. And the best candidate, party leaders agreed, was Franklin Delano Roosevelt.

When Smith first asked F.D.R. to run, he refused. "As I am only 46, I feel that I owe it to my family and myself to give the present constant improvement a chance to continue," Franklin explained. When other party leaders started calling him at Warm Springs, Franklin finally stopped answering the phone. He told his secretary to tell everyone that he had gone on a picnic. At last, Eleanor called. When she heard Franklin's voice on the line, she handed the phone to Smith.

"Frank, if we go ahead and nominate you, would you refuse to run?" Franklin hesitated for a moment. "Good," said Smith – and hung up.

The next day, the Democratic Party nominated Franklin Delano Roosevelt as its candidate for governor of New York. It was one of the few genuine "drafts" in American political history.

Chapter 5

Governor of New York

Although F.D.R. had been reluctant to run for the office of governor, once he was nominated he campaigned with his usual vigor and determination. In three weeks he traveled 1,300 miles and delivered as many as seven speeches a day. Most of the traveling was done in a touring car without a top, and he always spoke standing up in the back of the car.

When Republicans made pious statements about how difficult campaigning must be for "the unfortunate sick man," F.D.R. would respond by listing the number of miles he had traveled that day, the names of the towns he had visited, and the number of speeches he had made. "Too bad about the unfortunate sick man, isn't it?" And he would toss his head and flash a broad grin at the audience. People ate it up. They applauded his gallantry and turned out in record numbers to shake his hand.

Franklin thrived on the campaign. He enjoyed it so much, in fact, that he jokingly told friends that if it would only last for 12 months instead of three weeks, he would be able to throw away his cane for good!

On election night, the Roosevelt family gathered at the Biltmore Hotel in New York City to await the returns. They came in slowly over telegraph wires. (There were no computers or television in those days, and even radio was not yet widely used.) As might be expected, major attention focused on the presidential race. By 10:00 P.M. it was clear that Smith had lost, and badly. Southern states that had voted Democratic since the Civil War had gone over to Hoover. Smith was not even carrying his home state of New York.

The returns for governor came in more slowly. By 1:00 A.M., however, Franklin was so convinced that he too had lost the election that he went to bed. When he awoke the next morning, however, he learned he had been mistaken. During the night, the final returns had given him a margin of victory of 25,000 votes, less than one percent of the total.

A "ONE-HALF OF ONE PERCENT GOVERNOR"

Franklin Delano Roosevelt was sworn in as governor of New York on New Year's Day of 1929. He took the oath of office on the family Bible, which had been printed in Dutch in 1686. The ceremony was held in the same room in which Cousin Teddy had been sworn in as governor some 30 years earlier.

F.D.R.'s inaugural address called for an "era of good feeling." However, he soon found himself "in one continuous glorious fight with the Republican legislative leaders." Despite the opposition, he pushed hard in various areas and achieved some successes.

A Foretaste of the Future

Many of the programs and practices that Roosevelt pursued in Albany would later mark his presidency. His main emphasis as governor was on helping workers and farmers, many of whom were not sharing in the general prosperity. He supported old-age pensions, and he called for laws against child labor and for a 48-hour work week for women. He also advocated tax relief for small farmers, as well as the reforestation of abandoned farmland. And he fought for public development of hydroelectric facilities on the St. Lawrence River to provide cheaper electricity for upstate New York.

During this time, F.D.R. also began his practice of delivering "fireside chats." Whenever the state legislature balked at his ideas, he would take his message directly to the people by radio. He would explain what he was trying to do and what the obstacles were. Soon state legislators would find themselves overwhelmed with letters from their constituents. As Roosevelt observed, "It seems to me that radio is gradually bringing to the ears of our people matters of interest concerning their country which they refuse to consider in the daily press with their eyes." It was a new element in the American political process.

A conservative legislature was only one of the difficulties that F.D.R. faced. Another, surprisingly, was Al Smith, who could not understand how he had lost New York by more than 100,000 votes while F.D.R. had won it by 25,000 votes. He was convinced that his friend had somehow or other sold him out. To add to Smith's resentment, F.D.R. refused to keep most of Smith's appointees in office. He insisted on selecting his own staff and making his own plans. He was not going to be bossed, not even by the man he had twice nominated for the presidency.

Developing a Staff

The only official F.D.R. kept from Smith's regime was Frances Perkins, the head of the State Industrial Board. In fact, he not only kept Perkins, he promoted her to the post of state industrial commissioner. As such, she was responsible for enforcing all of the state's factory and labor laws. When Roosevelt became President, he chose Perkins as secretary of labor. She was our nation's first woman Cabinet member.

F.D.R. added to his staff several other people who were to play a large role in his presidency. There was Jim Farley, the state's boxing commissioner, who helped manage several of Roosevelt's presidential campaigns and served as postmaster general. There was "Sammy the Rose" Rosenman, who helped write Roosevelt's speeches and acted as his legal counsel.

There was also "Henry the Morgue" Morgenthau, Jr., a Dutchess County neighbor. One of F.D.R.'s techniques as governor was to appoint a group of experts to analyze a problem and to suggest several ways of handling it. Roosevelt appointed Morgenthau to head a committee of agricultural experts to see what could be done to help the dairy farmers of New York. Morgenthau later became secretary of the treasury.

F.D.R. did not limit himself to making good appointments. He spent a considerable amount of time traveling around New York by car, train, and even canalboat to see for himself what was going on. He was often accompanied by Eleanor, and whenever he visited a state hospital or prison, he would send her inside to look it over while he and the institution's superintendent talked.

One day, Franklin asked Eleanor what the inmates of a mental hospital were getting to eat. Eleanor handed him a copy of the menu. "But didn't you look into the pots on the stove?" he asked. Eleanor soon learned not only to look into pots but also to open closet doors, pull down bed covers, and question inmates. As a result, a number of state institutions were properly cleaned for the first time in years, while others were enlarged to prevent overcrowding.

THE CRASH OF '29

On October 24, 1929, a day known as "Black Thursday," the stock market collapsed. Prices plummeted to one-half their previous level, and millions of stockholders who had bought "on margin"—paying perhaps 10 percent down and owing the rest—were wiped out. Businesses lost billions of dollars worth of assets, and hundreds of banks failed.

As a result of the crash, people stopped buying anything that was not absolutely essential. When store owners saw that merchandise was piling up on their shelves, they stopped ordering goods and fired their clerks. With no orders coming in, factories closed and workers lost their jobs. Unemployment soared from four million to seven million almost overnight. It was the start of the worst economic depression in the nation's history.

In those years, there was no bank deposit insurance, no unemployment insurance, no public relief. If a bank failed, people simply lost all the money they had saved. If they were fired and could not find work, they had to depend on private organizations, like the Salvation Army, for a cup of soup or a slice of bread.

Conflicting Economic Theories

President Hoover subscribed to the prevailing notion of rugged individualism, which held that booms and depressions were a natural part of the economy. Nothing could or should be done about such "ups" and "downs" except to let them run their course. If people were hungry or homeless during the bad times, that was unfortunate. But they should rely on their own resourcefulness or the help of more fortunate individuals. If the government were to help in any way, it would be considered socialism.

Roosevelt, however, felt differently. To him, the people who were being hurt by the Great Depression were like the polio victims he had met at Warm Springs. They were suffering because of something over which they had no control. In his opinion, those who were not suffering had an obligation to help those who were, "not as a matter of charity, but as a matter of *social duty.*" If people lost their means of livelihood, then it was the responsibility of the government to step in. "The duty of the state toward the citizens is the duty of the servant to his master," Roosevelt said.

A Series of Experiments

Roosevelt did not have a broad theoretical program in mind to help the people in his state. What he did have was the will to try a number of innovative projects, some of which he felt sure would work. "It is time we experimented," he declared. "Please do not dismiss these ideas with the word radical. Remember the radical of yesterday is almost [always] the reactionary of today."

Roosevelt began by trying to stabilize unemployment through such techniques as shortening the work week for women and eliminating child labor. He was also the first governor in the nation to propose a system of unemployment insurance.

After he was re-elected governor in 1930 by a tremendous margin of 725,000 votes, F.D.R. proposed the first direct relief program in the country. Known as the Temporary Emergency Relief Administration, or TERA, it used state funds to put people to work on public projects. Soon thousands of New Yorkers were busy building parks, roads, schools, and reservoirs. TERA eventually helped about 40 percent of the state's population.

Opponents of the TERA program called it "leaf-raking," and F.D.R. acknowledged that it was only a stop-gap measure. But to those involved, it was a means both of earning some money and of keeping their self-respect. Roosevelt appointed a young social worker from Iowa named Harry L. Hopkins to head the agency. Like Louis Howe, Hopkins was to remain totally devoted to F.D.R. for the rest of his life.

"NO LONGER AMERICA"

By 1932 economic conditions in the United States had become so bad that many people feared the country was on the verge of revolution. Unemployment had doubled, from seven million to 14 million. On many street corners, men stood selling apples for five cents each. Some 9 million bank accounts had been wiped out. Many schools had closed because there were no funds to pay teachers. There were often no funds to pay police officers or fire fighters either. Groups of tarpaper shacks, called "Hoovervilles," sprang up in vacant lots at the edges of most cities and became home to people who had been evicted from their residences for not paying their rent or their mortgage.

Farmers in such conservative states as Iowa, Minnesota, and Nebraska declared a "farm holiday." Instead of selling food for less than it cost to produce, they poured milk on the ground and slaughtered their cattle. In Virginia, starving miners smashed grocery store windows to get food. In Michigan, factory guards fired machine guns at a parade of jobless workers, killing four. And in Washington, D.C., veterans of World War I who were petitioning Congress to pay them a promised bonus ahead of schedule were forcibly driven out of the city. "What a pitiful spectacle is that of the great American Government, mightiest in the world, chasing unarmed men, women and children with Army tanks," observed a local newspaper. "If the Army must be called out to make war on unarmed citizens, this is no longer America."

As matters worsened, F.D.R. kept speaking out boldly. "The situation is serious, and the time has come for us to

Sights such as this unemployed worker standing hopelessly outside a vacant store were common throughout the United States during the Great Depression. (Franklin D. Roosevelt Library.)

face this unpleasant fact dispassionately and constructively as a scientist faces a test tube of deadly germs." The economy was sick, he continued, and the American people had to find a cure. Roosevelt believed that a government's justification for existing was to serve and protect the people, not to stand idly on the sidelines. "The country needs . . . the country demands bold, persistent experimentation. . . . Above all, try something. . . . The millions who are in want will not stand silently by forever while the things to satisfy their needs are within easy reach."

THE 1932 DEMOCRATIC CONVENTION

On January 23, 1932, one week before his 50th birthday, Franklin Delano Roosevelt announced his candidacy for the Democratic nomination for President. He immediately began putting together a team of advisors known as the Brain Trust, which included several professors from Columbia University in addition to such veterans as Louis Howe and Harry Hopkins. It was the Brain Trust's responsibility to come up with detailed information on specific problems, to suggest policies, and to write first drafts of F.D.R.'s speeches. Roosevelt would then dictate his own speech, using the first draft for reference.

A Gaggle of Candidates

The 1932 presidential race attracted a large number of other Democratic candidates for the nomination. Unlike 1928, 1932 looked like an excellent year for the Democrats. Many Americans felt that even if the Republicans had not caused the Depression, they certainly had done nothing to end it. So in state after state, senators and governors began presenting themselves as "favorite sons," whose state delegation would vote for them on the first ballot.

Roosevelt's main opponent, however, was Alfred E. Smith, who felt that as the party's standard bearer in 1928, he deserved the nomination again. Besides, Smith was still bitter about F.D.R.'s failure as governor to keep his appointees and follow his advice. If Roosevelt went to Washington, he might continue to ignore loyal party regulars. Moreover, Smith and his big business supporters were frightened by some of F.D.R.'s speeches. What did he mean by saying that the outlook of certain businessmen was "[colored] by the fact that they can make huge profits"? What was this talk that prosperity depended on "the forgotten man at the bottom of the economic pyramid"? To Smith, it seemed as if F.D.R. was "setting class against class."

All through the winter and spring of 1932, "Frank" and "Al" battled tooth and nail for delegates. When the Democratic National Convention opened in Chicago on June 27, F.D.R. had 666¼ of the 770 votes needed for the nomination. Smith had 201¾ votes. Three major favorite sons controlled 200 votes between them; a number of minor favorite sons held the rest.

Making a Deal

In Albany, Franklin, Eleanor, Sara, and sons Elliott and John gathered in the living room of the governor's mansion to listen to the convention by radio. Telephone and telegraph wires and a radio were also installed in the garage, where newspaper reporters had set up shop. They reported that the governor "was calm and cheerful" and that "Mrs. Roosevelt was knitting." Other members of the family, as well as Louis Howe and James Farley, were in Chicago.

The actual balloting did not begin until early morning on July 1. After three roll calls, the tally stood at 683 votes for F.D.R. and 190¼ for Smith, almost unchanged from the first ballot. Party leaders were very upset. The last thing they wanted was a repetition of the deadlocked 1924 convention with its 103 ballots. So they adjourned until evening—and Howe and Farley worked out a deal. If the Texas and California delegates would switch from favorite son John Nance Garner of Texas, F.D.R. would choose Garner as his running mate. Texas and California agreed—and the bandwagon began to roll.

That evening, Roosevelt was nominated on the fourth ballot by 945 votes to Smith's 190 votes. The band struck up "Happy Days Are Here Again," which was to become F.D.R.'s campaign song. And in Albany, the presidential candidate scooted happily around the room in his wheelchair as flash bulbs exploded, people flung pieces of paper into the air, and automobile horns honked loudly in the street outside.

Breaking with Tradition

Until 1932, it had been the custom for a party's presidential nominee to pretend that he knew nothing about what had happened at the convention until he was formally notified two or three weeks later by an official committee. To F.D.R., that seemed silly and hypocritical. Besides, since he was advocating the use of bold new ideas to fight the Depression, it seemed appropriate to kick off his campaign in a bold new way.

So together with Eleanor, sons Elliott and John, his staff, and his bodyguards, Roosevelt boarded a plane and flew to Chicago to accept the nomination in person. Because flying was still a novelty in those days, the convention delegates listened intently to radio reports of F.D.R.'s progress. The plane ran into heavy winds, it had to stop to refuel, and it landed several hours behind schedule. But as Roosevelt moved slowly to the platform on the arm of his son James, an electric excitement gripped the convention.

"I appreciate your willingness after these six arduous days to remain here," he began in his golden-rich voice. "The appearance before a National Convention of its nominee for President . . . is unprecedented and unusual, but these are unprecedented and unusual times. Let it be from now on the task of our party to break foolish traditions." He continued by attacking the Republicans for their lack of leadership and urged his fellow Democrats to push forward a program of recovery. "Ours must be a party of liberal thought, of planned action, of enlightened international outlook, and of the greatest good to the greatest number of our citizens." After outlining some of his proposals for social and economic change, he concluded: "I pledge you, I pledge myself, to a new deal for the American people." The phrase "New Deal" was later ap-

The foaming mug of beer on this license plate reminded voters that the repeal of Prohibition was one of the planks in the 1932 platform of the Democratic Party. (Franklin D. Roosevelt Library.)

plied to the laws about economic recovery and reform that were passed during F.D.R.'s presidency.

ON THE CAMPAIGN TRAIL

The Republicans chose President Herbert Hoover to face Roosevelt in the election. The personal contrast between the two candidates was as striking as their political differences. The President looked grim, exhausted, and depressed. As one observer commented, "If you put a rose in Hoover's hand it would wilt." Roosevelt, on the other hand, radiated confidence and vitality. At every stop of his campaign train, "The Roosevelt Special," he would appear on the rear platform, smile and wave enthusiastically at his audience, and shake hands warmly with as many people as could reach him.

Roosevelt covered some 27,000 miles on his campaign trip. Every few days he made a major speech on general policy. In between, he delivered hundreds of informal talks on matters of local concern. As he had when he ran his first campaign for state senator, Roosevelt concentrated on the farmers. Although Farm Belt voters were traditionally Republican, F.D.R. believed he could win them over. As a farmer himself, he knew their problems and could discuss them in simple, direct language.

Actually, many of F.D.R.'s speeches were somewhat vague. He and his Brain Trust were still developing the New Deal program. Moreover, he did not want to antagonize too many voters with specific details. What he *did* want was to give the American people a sense of hope and of dedication to a cause. "This is more than a political campaign; it is a call to arms," Roosevelt said. "Give me your help, not to win votes alone, but to win in this crusade to restore America to its own people."

The election results were a landslide for Roosevelt, who

carried 42 states to Hoover's 6, winning 472 electoral votes to Hoover's 59. It was the most lopsided victory of any presidential election to that time.

AN ASSASSINATION ATTEMPT

Before the passage of the 20th Amendment in 1933, a President elected in November did not take office until the following March. So F.D.R. spent the next several months in Warm Springs working out the details of his New Deal and choosing members of his Cabinet.

In mid-February, Roosevelt stopped in Miami, Florida, to say a few words at an American Legion meeting. During the speech, a large crowd gathered in the street to see the future President. As F.D.R. moved through the crowd waving and smiling from his automobile, an unemployed bricklayer named Giuseppe Zangara leaped toward the car shouting, "I hate all rulers! I hate all rich and powerful men! Kings! Bankers! Presidents!"

Zangara pulled a gun and began to fire. The shots missed the President-elect, but Chicago Mayor Anton Cermak, who was riding in the car with F.D.R., slumped over in the seat next to Roosevelt. "I'm mighty glad it was me instead of you," Cermak whispered. He died of his wounds the next day. Four other members of F.D.R.'s party were injured.

INAUGURATION DAY

Saturday, March 4, 1933, started out cold and rainy in Washington, D.C. In the morning, the Roosevelts attended services at St. John's Episcopal Church, not far from the White House. Later in the day, the weather cleared as F.D.R.

and Hoover rode in an open car along Pennsylvania Avenue to the Capitol, where the oath of office was to be administered.

The retiring President rode in silence, so F.D.R. did too. But as they moved through the cheering crowd of some 650,000 spectators, the President-elect began to lose patience. "I said to myself, 'Spinach! Protocol or no protocol, somebody has to do something.' The two of us simply couldn't sit there on our hands, ignoring each other and everyone else. So I began to wave my own response with my top hat and I kept waving it until I got to the inauguration stand and was sworn in."

Franklin Delano Roosevelt took the oath of office as the nation's 32nd President on the same family Bible on which he had been sworn in as governor of New York. Instead of calling for "an era of good feeling," however, his inaugural address was a trumpet call to battle. "This nation asks for action, and action now!" he declared. The United States, he said, was engaged in a war against the Great Depression, and he intended to wage that war as "if we were in fact invaded by a foreign foe. . . . The people of the United States . . . in their need" had chosen him to lead the fight against fear, hunger, and unemployment. "In the spirit of the gift, I take it," he stated. ". . . May God guide me in the days to come."

The next morning, humorist and political commentator Will Rogers wrote in his column: "America hasn't been as happy in three years as they are today. No money, no banks, no work, no nothing, but they know they got a man in there who is wise to Congress, wise to our so-called big men. The whole country is with him."

Chapter 6

The New Deal: Part One

No sooner was Roosevelt inaugurated as President than he called Congress into special session. During the 100 days the session lasted, from March 9 to June 16, 1933, he proposed one bill after another—and Congress agreed to every one. Not since the United States' first year as an independent nation were so many important laws passed in such a short period of time.

A BANK HOLIDAY

Even before Congress met, Roosevelt moved into action. With a stroke of the pen, he closed every bank in the United States for a week. The purpose of the bank holiday was to prevent total collapse of the country's monetary system.

During the four months between F.D.R.'s election and his inauguration, a terrible banking crisis had developed. True, banks had been failing ever since the Depression started. Many of them had issued unsafe mortgages and other loans, and when people were no longer able to repay, these banks failed. But in February 1933, sound banks also began failing.

All of a sudden rumors began to spread around the country that there was no more cash left in the banking system.

Alarmed depositors rushed to take out their savings. They did not realize that since banks invest most of the money people deposit with them, they would be forced to close their doors if too many depositors wanted their money back at the same time. Lines began forming hours before the start of a business day. In many cases, the run on banks was so great that police had to be called in to keep order.

Even withdrawing cash from a bank did not mean that a person's money was safe. A rash of holdups broke out. But as one police captain said unhappily, "There's nothing we can do about it. My men can't escort everyone home. All the crooks have to do is watch and see who comes out of the bank and then follow him. It's a mess!"

During the bank holiday, no one had much cash on hand. There were no credit cards in those days, so stores, movie houses, restaurants, and hotels posted signs reading "DON'T WORRY ABOUT THE CASH! WE'LL TAKE YOUR CHECK." In general, people responded with good humor and a sense that at last something was being done.

Indeed, something was being done. During the bank holiday, all the nation's banks were examined by auditors. Those that were found to be in sound financial condition—about three out of four—were allowed to reopen. Those that were financially unsound remained closed. As a result, people regained confidence in the banking system and deposits began to rise.

The people's confidence was strengthened by the first of President Roosevelt's fireside chats to the nation. Opening with the words "My friends and fellow Americans," he described what he had done and why. As Will Rogers said, F.D.R. explained banking so clearly that he "made everybody understand it, even the bankers." Two days after the banks reopened, the stock market went up.

Toward the end of the Hundred Days, Congress passed a law that made the banking system much safer for the average person. The law set up the Federal Deposit Insurance Corporation (FDIC) to insure savings accounts of up to $5,000 against bank failures. Today, federal insurance protects each bank account up to $100,000.

RELIEF AND RECOVERY

In his inaugural address, Roosevelt declared that "Our greatest primary task is to put people to work." In March 1933, that meant creating jobs for 15 million unemployed Americans.

The CCC

The first job program was one of Roosevelt's favorite projects. It was called the Civilian Conservation Corps, or CCC, and it not only created jobs but also helped preserve the nation's natural resources of forests, land, and animals.

Since the start of the Great Depression, thousands of men in their late teens and early 20s had been wandering around the country, riding freight trains from town to town, and often drifting into crime. The CCC put these men to work in camps in the woods. Many of them came from city slums and had never seen mountains or slept in the fresh air before.

Under the direction of forestry experts, the young men planted more than 200 million trees in a great belt from Canada to Mexico. The belt of trees kept the soil on the Great Plains from being blown away by the wind. The men also built truck trails and irrigation dams, and they restocked national parks with fish and game. In exchange, they received room, board, uniforms of forest green, and $30 a month, part of which they had to send home to their families. In addition to work, there was time for play and study. The camps provided books, newspapers, vocational training, and courses in debating and dramatics.

At its busiest, the CCC employed half a million workers. By the time it ended in 1941, almost three million young men had passed through the camps. Critics of the program called it "forced labor." But to Roosevelt, these young men were soldiers in the war against the Depression.

The CWA

The second job program that F.D.R. proposed was the Civil Works Administration, or CWA. This program was an outgrowth of the Federal Emergency Relief Administration, or FERA, which had been designed to rush federal funds to states and cities to feed the hungry. Its director was Harry Hopkins, who had done a similar job for F.D.R. in the state of New York. Hopkins, however, had been a social worker before joining Roosevelt's staff, and he knew that most people would rather work than accept charity. When he discussed the matter with the President, F.D.R. agreed and told Hopkins to "invent four million jobs in thirty days."

In less than a month, Hopkins created 4,264,000 jobs. The CWA hired workers to build roads, schools, airports, playgrounds, and athletic fields. CWA teachers gave adult education courses or worked in rural schools that would otherwise have been closed for lack of funds. CWA writers produced histories of every state in the Union, and CWA seamstresses turned surplus cotton into mattresses for the poor. All in all, the CWA program of work relief turned out to be one of the best morale builders of the New Deal.

Alphabet Soup

The FDIC, CCC, and CWA were only three of the New Deal agencies that people were soon referring to as alphabet soup. Eight were established during the Hundred Days, and another ten over the next five years. They were designed to help as many different groups as possible, for F.D.R. considered himself the President of *all* the people.

Accordingly, the Home Owners Loan Corporation (HOLC) helped nonfarm homeowners keep their homes by refinancing their mortgages at low interest rates and by letting them borrow money for taxes and repairs. The Securities and Exchange Commission (SEC) protected stockholders by requiring companies to give investors information about their stock. The Agricultural Adjustment Administration (AAA) was aimed at farmers, whom it paid to cut back on the production of certain crops that were in oversupply. As production declined, the price for these crops went up, which meant that the farmers had more money to spend.

Business people and factory workers were not left out either. The National Recovery Administration (NRA) was, according to F.D.R., "the most important and far-reaching" agency yet established. It administered industry-wide codes of fair practices that were drafted by management and labor together. Employers agreed to minimum wages of 30 to 40 cents an hour, a maximum work week of 40 hours, and an end to child labor. Employees agreed to share the work by giving up one or two days a week so that unemployed persons could have part-time jobs.

The NRA was headed by General Hugo "Ironpants" Johnson, who designed the agency's symbol of a Blue Eagle with the slogan "We Do Our Part." Soon store windows everywhere were displaying Blue Eagle posters, and housewives were buying only goods that carried the Blue Eagle stamp. Eventually, two million employers and 23 million workers were covered by NRA codes.

CHANGES IN WASHINGTON

Roosevelt's energy and enthusiasm were reflected in the nation's capital. The people who rushed there to work in New Deal agencies were different from the stodgy politicians who had held down jobs under the three previous administrations. The New Dealers were mostly young, bright-eyed, and full of ideas. They hounded Postmaster General Farley, who administered patronage, "like wolves on the prowl." When they were hired, they worked late every night.

There were physical changes in the nation's capital as well. Because the new agencies needed room, office buildings were soon rising everywhere, and bricklayers, electricians, and others who had been unemployed just months before found themselves working overtime.

There was a physical change in the White House, too. Roosevelt had a swimming pool installed in the building's west terrace so that he could continue with his swimming exercises.

Both the President and Mrs. Roosevelt favored a casual life style. There were grandchildren and dogs all over the White House, and Eleanor would sometimes help the servants move furniture around. If someone protested that such a thing wasn't done by a First Lady, she simply replied, "It is now."

Those Roosevelt children still at home were equally casual. They raided the refrigerator at all hours, and once were almost locked out all night because they forgot to carry their identification with them.

Although F.D.R. was calling for large expenditures of federal funds, he was rather frugal at home. He wore his jackets until they fell apart, and he bought no more than two new pairs of shoes a year. He kept the battered felt hat he had worn during his 1920 vice-presidential campaign, his excuse being that it brought him good luck. And he boasted that when he sliced turkey, it was so thin one could "almost *read* through it!"

In addition to swimming in the White House pool, F.D.R. relaxed by playing poker, sailing on the Potomac River, and working on his stamp collection. He had an advantage as President. Each week, he had the State Department send him a bag of foreign stamps from its correspondence around the world.

A HARD-WORKING CHIEF EXECUTIVE

President Roosevelt usually ate breakfast in bed, during which time he read the newspapers, planned his program for the day, and listened to reports from Eleanor, who traveled around the country to find out firsthand what was going on. By 10 o'clock, he was at his desk in the Oval Office.

Appointments and conferences took up much of the day. Roosevelt also spent several hours each day on the phone, coaxing members of Congress to vote the way he wanted and arranging political deals. In the late afternoon, he would ring for his secretary and dictate replies to important letters, of which there were literally hundreds. Every time his secretary entered with an armful of correspondence, he would ask hopefully, "Is that all we have to do?" And every time she would reply, "No, sir. This is all I could carry. There is more coming up."

After dinner, Roosevelt again worked at his desk until 11 or 12 at night. And sometimes he took letters and documents to bed with him to read before falling asleep.

Despite his long hours, the President remained in excellent health. He swam almost every day, and a personal physician checked him almost every morning and every evening. He bristled with so much energy, in fact, that aides referred to him as "a human dynamo." Those who could not keep up with him were soon dropped.

Like the New Deal itself, Roosevelt's Cabinet meetings were markedly different from those of previous Presidents. For one thing, he chose people from a variety of backgrounds. In addition to the first woman Cabinet member, there were both northerners and southerners, conservatives as well as liberals, and even some Republicans.

Roosevelt encouraged his Cabinet members to express their opinions and argue about their differences. He would sometimes assign the same goal to two different people to see what they would do. At the same time, when a decision was called for, there was no doubt where the President stood. "When he wants something a lot," observed a White House aide, "he can be formidable—when crossed he is hard, stubborn, resourceful, relentless."

Roosevelt consulted frequently with members of Congress. He was charming, genial, and a "soft" persuader. Instead of antagonizing opponents by declaring bluntly that they were against him, he would say graciously, "You are not with me today. But tomorrow we shall look at the matter again. Perhaps we shall then see it from a different angle and under a different light."

The White House guest list reflected F.D.R.'s belief that he was the President of *all* the people. He welcomed members of racial and religious minorities, as well as labor leaders and college professors. He invited authors, artists, and movie actresses to dinner or tea. Previous administrations had usually ignored these groups.

Roosevelt made great use of press conferences. He held them twice a week, and generally answered reporters' questions in a frank and open manner. He knew most reporters by their first names and kidded them as if they were family. "Will reporters be allowed to use the new swimming pool and play tennis on the White House courts?" a newsman once asked F.D.R. "Of course," Roosevelt replied, "and the children have a sandpile. You boys can play in it, if you like."

Most of all, the President used his fireside chats on the radio to explain his program to the people and ask for their help and trust. And the people responded. After his first fireside chat, for instance, more than half a million letters flooded the White House in just one week.

Chapter 7

The New Deal: Part Two

Halfway through his first term, Roosevelt decided to change course. Instead of emphasizing short-term measures for relief and recovery, he was going to push for long-term reforms. Although by now it was clear that the country would survive the economic crisis, there were still some 10 million Americans who were unemployed. So why not try a new strategy?

As the President's reforms went into effect, they were sharply criticized from both political right (conservatives) and left (liberals). The right felt that "King Franklin" was going too far, while the left felt that he was not going far enough. To big business, "that Red in the White House" was, if not actually a communist, then pretty close to one. To communists, socialists, and radicals like the followers of Senator Huey Long of Louisiana, F.D.R. was "a social Fascist."

Roosevelt was none of these, of course. He simply believed that some middle-of-the-road adjustments needed to be made in the nation's economic system. With one exception, all the reforms he proposed are still part of the American scene.

THE TVA

The Tennessee Valley Authority, or TVA, had actually been established during the Hundred Days. However, it was really a reform measure. Its aim was to develop an entire region through its water resources.

On his way to and from Warm Springs, Roosevelt had driven several times through parts of the Tennessee Valley. About three-fourths the size of England, the region was one of the most poverty-stricken in the country. Over the years, the original forests had been cut down, causing much of the topsoil to be eroded by floods. Now, it was hard for farmers to grow crops.

In 1917 the federal government had built a dam at Muscle Shoals, Alabama. Electricity from the dam was used to produce nitrates for munitions. After World War I, Senator George Norris of Nebraska urged that the dam be used for flood control and that the nitrates be made into fertilizer. The first bill that Norris got through Congress was vetoed by President Coolidge; the second, by President Hoover.

The third time, Senator Norris had far better luck. Roosevelt not only approved of the idea, he expanded upon it. He suggested a series of dams through the entire valley. They would control floods and create lakes for fishing, swimming, and boating. They would also produce electricity for factories and homes. Moreover, the price of the electricity would set a "yardstick" against which people could measure the rates that private power companies in the region were charging. Roosevelt was angry about his high electric bills at Warm Springs. The trouble, he felt, was that there was no competition around, so the private electrical companies could charge anything they pleased.

The private companies fought back, all the way to the Supreme Court. But F.D.R. won the battle, and the Tennes-

Only two out of every hundred farms in the Tennessee Valley had electricity before TVA dams such as this one were built. (Franklin D. Roosevelt Library.)

see River was harnessed. When Eleanor Roosevelt visited the region just eight years later, she reported that "a more prosperous area would have been hard to find." The TVA has since become a model for the development of river valleys all around the world.

THE WPA

Despite its success in providing more than four million part-time jobs, the CWA came in for a great deal of criticism, some of it justified. The money that local officials received was not always properly administered, and many small-time politicians diverted federal funds into their own pockets and those of their friends. Then, too, some CWA projects—like studying the history of the safety pin—were "boondoggles," or make-work projects. Something more substantial was needed.

So Roosevelt ended the CWA and proposed a new jobs program instead, the Works Projects Administration, or WPA. This program was designed to do two things: to build large construction projects, and to hire skilled workers for jobs in their own trades. Opponents of the program warned that people on WPA would be loafers, not laborers, and that WPA stood for "Won't Produce Anything."

In reality, WPA workers produced a great deal. They built New York City's La Guardia Airport and the St. Louis waterfront, as well as thousands of schools, hospitals, bridges, and roads. They cleaned up slums and parks all over the country. WPA artists painted murals on post offices and other public buildings, and WPA musicians gave free public concerts. WPA actors put on free dramatic productions for people who had never seen a play in their lives. The plays were presented in several foreign languages as well as in English. Many of the writers employed on the Federal Writers' Project—like Nelson Algren, Saul Bellow, John Cheever, and Richard Wright—later became quite famous.

Also under the WPA was the National Youth Administration (NYA), which gave part-time employment to more than two million high school and college students so they could continue their education. It also provided vocational training for over 2½ million idle young people who were not attending school. Roosevelt had always insisted that help be given to everyone regardless of race or religion. Accordingly, he appointed Mary McLeod Bethune to head the NYA's Division of Negro Affairs. Bethune was the first black woman to be in charge of a federal agency.

In general, the WPA was efficiently and honestly run. Altogether, it provided jobs for 8½ million Americans. It went out of existence in 1943, after the booming economy of World War II finally ended unemployment.

THE WAGNER ACT

Prior to the New Deal, the federal government had almost always supported management against labor. To F.D.R., this did not seem fair. If the government were to be truly a government for *all* the people, then workers were entitled to as much protection as employers.

At the President's urging, Congress passed the National Labor Relations Act, commonly known as the Wagner Act after its sponsor, Senator Robert Wagner of New York. The act required employers to bargain with their workers over wages, hours, and working conditions. Moreover, companies could no longer fire workers for joining a union. The act set up a National Labor Relations Board (NLRB) to hold elections for workers to choose the union (if any) that they wanted, and to hear complaints by workers about unfair labor practices.

Employers fought hard against the Wagner Act at first. But the Supreme Court agreed with F.D.R. that workers had the right to bargain collectively with management. As a result, labor unions began to grow, especially in such mass-production industries as steel and automobiles. The Wagner Act, with some amendments, is still in effect.

SOCIAL SECURITY

The fourth major reform bill that F.D.R. had enacted was the most far-reaching of all.

The story goes that Dr. Francis E. Townsend, a public health official in California, saw three old women picking through a garbage pail for scraps of food. When he reported the incident in the press, it created a national sensation. Dr. Townsend then launched a crusade to have the federal government pay a monthly pension of $200 to everyone over age 65. The only condition was that the recipient had to spend the $200 within 30 days, which would help business. The money for the pensions would come from a national sales tax.

Economists pointed out that the "Townsend Plan" would give 50 percent of the nation's income to only 10 percent of the people. Nevertheless, the idea spread rapidly; soon there were more than 2,000 Townsend Clubs in the country.

As governor of New York, F.D.R. had fought for a system of old-age pensions. Now, he appointed a committee of experts to examine the problem from a national perspective. After studying the committee's report, he proposed that Congress set up a system of old-age insurance. That way, old people would not have to depend on charity.

Under the Social Security Act of 1935, both employers and employees pay an equal tax on wages. The money collected is then paid out to the workers when they retire, usually at the age of 65. The act also provides for aid to the blind, the disabled, dependent mothers, neglected children, and the needy elderly. Today, Social Security touches the lives of more Americans than any other New Deal reform.

"THE BLIZZARD OF '36"

By 1936 the United States was very different from what it had been four years earlier. Banks were no longer failing; the Hoovervilles were nearly deserted. Although nine million Americans were still out of work, unemployment had been lowered by six million, and more jobs were opening up every day. The five-day work week was standard, and child labor was becoming a thing of the past. The gross national product had grown by 40 percent as factories resumed operations and farmers replanted their fields.

Even more important than the improvements in the national economy was the change in the attitude of the American people. Gone was all talk of revolution. In place of despair and fear, there was now hope and determination.

After he was renominated by acclamation at the 1936 Democratic National Convention, Roosevelt gave an acceptance speech in which he listed the accomplishments of the New Deal and the challenges of the future:

> Governments can err. Presidents do make mistakes but . . . better the occasional faults of a Government that lives in a spirit of charity than the consistent omission of a Government frozen in the ice of its own indifference. . . . There is a mysterious cycle in human events. To some generations much is given. Of other generations much is expected. This generation of Americans have a rendezvous with destiny.

For their presidential candidate, the Republicans nominated Governor Alf Landon of Kansas, a pleasant if rather colorless individual. Although the Republican platform kept such New Deal reforms as old-age benefits and public works, many of Landon's supporters launched into a vicious personal attack on F.D.R. He had allowed the Democratic Party to be "seized by alien and un-American elements." He had suffered a stroke. He had had a series of heart attacks. He was losing his mind. He had been found "shrieking like a maniac in the middle of the night, and it had required the combined efforts of several attendants to control him." The malicious comments went on and on.

On election day there was an avalanche of votes in favor of the New Deal. F.D.R. carried every state except Maine and Vermont. His popular vote stood at 27,752,869 to Landon's 16,674,665 — the biggest margin yet in a presidential election. His electoral vote of 523 to 8 represented the greatest plurality since 1820. In addition, the Democrats captured both houses of Congress by the biggest majorities since 1869.

The 1936 election was so overwhelmingly one-sided that it was called "The Blizzard of '36." It was a moment of supreme triumph for President Roosevelt. But as matters turned out, it was also the start of four years of troubles.

Chapter **8**

The New Deal Winds Down

Under the newly ratified 20th Amendment, Roosevelt's second inauguration took place in January instead of March. For the week preceding January 20, the entire eastern half of the country had been suffering from a deluge of rain, and Inauguration Day was no exception. The sky dripped steadily, a gusty wind tore at people's umbrellas, and the Marine Corps band barely managed to play "Hail to the Chief" because so much rainwater kept getting into their instruments.

Despite the downpour, Roosevelt took the oath bareheaded. He then delivered another of his moving and memorable orations. "Our progress out of the Depression is obvious," he declared. America was at last making its way along "the road of enduring progress." But the war had not yet been won. "I see one-third of a nation ill-housed, ill-clad, ill-nourished," he stated. He called on the American people once again to join him in the struggle. "The test of our progress is not whether we add more to the abundance of those who have much; it is whether we provide enough for those who have too little."

THE COURT-PACKING PLAN

On February 5, less than three weeks after his inauguration, President Roosevelt dropped a political bombshell. He presented Congress with a plan to reorganize the Supreme Court. Under the terms of the proposed law, if a justice did not retire within six months of his 70th birthday, a President would be allowed to appoint a new justice, up to a maximum of six. That would raise to 15 the total number of justices on the Supreme Court. What the proposed law meant in practice was that Roosevelt would be able to appoint six new justices at once, because two-thirds of the Supreme Court's members were then over age 70.

Roosevelt's Reason

There was a reason for Roosevelt's proposal. In May 1935 the Supreme Court had declared the National Recovery Administration unconstitutional on the ground that it gave the President too much power. The Court also stated that Congress had gone too far in regulating industry. The decision shocked F.D.R., who criticized the Court for its "horse-and-buggy definition of interstate commerce."

Then, in January 1936, the Supreme Court struck down the Agricultural Adjustment Administration. It held that Congress had again exceeded its legislative authority. This convinced Roosevelt that the justices were out of touch with reality. Their conservative interpretation of the Constitution might have been acceptable half a century earlier, when they were in law school, but it was much too far removed from the realities of the 1930s. How could the "physical conditions of 1787 in farming, labor, manufacturing, mining, industry, and finance" be considered the "yardsticks of legal power" some 150 years later? The issue, in the President's words, was "whether the kind of government which the people of the United States had voted for in 1932, 1934, and 1936 was to be permitted by the Supreme Court to function."

Roosevelt pointed out that the size of the Supreme Court had been changed six times before during the nation's history. Besides, "the laws of many states, the practice of the Civil Service, the regulations of the Army and Navy, and the rules of many of our universities and of almost every great private business enterprise, commonly fix the retirement age at seventy years or less."

Popular Objections

Roosevelt may have been right in most of his arguments. Nevertheless, the Supreme Court proposal was perhaps the worst blunder of his political career. Dozens of lawyers, historians, and government experts argued that he was violating the traditional separation of powers between the executive, legislative, and judicial branches of government. Republicans accused F.D.R. of trying to become a dictator by "loading" the Court with "flunkies of his own choosing." Democrats felt that he was simply avenging himself on the Court for its anti-New Deal decisions. Thousands of protesting letters poured into Congress.

Roosevelt fought back. He compared the government to a three-horse team, and urged that "[we] not permit one of the horses to fall behind the other two." He argued that the "nine old men" of the Supreme Court were substituting their own economic opinions for those of a Congress elected by the people. But opposition to Roosevelt's proposal continued.

Then, in April 1936, the Supreme Court took some of the wind out of F.D.R.'s sails by approving the National Labor Relations Act. Later that same month, it upheld the constitutionality of the Social Security Act. In May Justice Willis Van Devanter, who had turned 78, announced his retirement from the bench, thus enabling Roosevelt to appoint a liberal judge in his place. In August Congress adjourned – and that was the end of the Court-packing plan.

A SENSE OF HUMOR

The fight over the Supreme Court dealt a serious blow to Roosevelt's prestige. Yet through it all, the President kept his sense of humor. For example, one day Mrs. Roosevelt left the White House early in the morning to visit a Baltimore prison as part of her survey of the federal prison system. When F.D.R. asked Eleanor's secretary where his wife was, the secretary replied, "She is in prison, Mr. President." "I'm not surprised," retorted F.D.R., "but what for?"

Like many self-confident individuals, Roosevelt was always telling jokes on himself. His favorite story was about a commuter from the Republican stronghold of Westchester County, New York. Every morning on the way to his office, the man would walk into the railroad station, hand the newsboy a quarter, pick up the *New York Herald Tribune,* glance at the front page, and then return the paper before rushing off to catch his train. Finally the newsboy, unable to hold back his curiosity any longer, asked the customer why he did that. "I'm interested in the obituary notices," the man replied. "But, sir, they're way over on page 24." "Boy, the [scoundrel] *I* want to see dead will be on page one!"

Then there was F.D.R.'s favorite cartoon. It showed a little girl running to tell her mother, who was standing in front of a large and elegant house, "Look, mama, Wilfred wrote a bad word!" The word on the sidewalk was "Roosevelt."

THE MARCH OF DIMES

In a more serious vein, F.D.R. spent a great deal of time setting up an organization to fight infantile paralysis. He wanted to use his upcoming 56th birthday to kick off a campaign for funds. A friend of his, comedian Eddie Cantor, suggested a 30-second appeal over all the national radio programs originating from Hollywood. People could be encouraged to send money, even if it were only a dime, directly to the White House, Cantor said. But the campaign needed a catchy slogan. "We could call it the March of Dimes," suggested Cantor.

Roosevelt liked Cantor's idea, and the first March of Dimes campaign was launched on the President's birthday, January 30, 1938. The next morning, 30,000 letters containing money arrived at the White House. The letters and contributions continued at such a rate that White House secretaries were soon joking that it was impossible to find the official mail.

That year alone, three new buildings for polio victims were constructed at Warm Springs. The chapel—where Catholic, Protestant, and Jewish services alike were conducted—had a special design. There were only a few pews but lots of room for stretchers and wheelchairs. The new school and library enabled youngsters to continue their education while getting treatment. A medical building provided operating rooms and other orthopedic facilities.

The next year, a brace shop was opened. It not only sold orthopedic appliances but also designed and tested new ones. One of its customers was F.D.R., who replaced his 40-pound leg braces with lighter ones that weighed only 20 pounds.

THE END OF THE NEW DEAL

The fight over the Supreme Court had pushed reform legislation to the sidelines. In addition, Democratic members of Congress who disagreed with Roosevelt's economic ideas began to speak out more forcefully against them. Nevertheless, several additional New Deal measures were passed in 1938. They included the Second Agricultural Adjustment Act, which guaranteed prices for certain farm commodities, and the Fair

Labor Standards Act, which established a minimum wage and a maximum work week for the nation.

When the 1938 congressional elections rolled around, F.D.R. decided to take an active role in the campaign. He hoped to get rid of those Democrats who had opposed his program from the start. But once again, he misjudged the situation. For one thing, voters often resent a President's interference in local elections. Even F.D.R., when he ran for re-election as governor of New York in 1930, had criticized President Hoover for sending in Cabinet members to speak against him. Then, too, the fight over the Supreme Court had seriously hurt F.D.R.'s popularity and political clout. It left him wide open to accusations of trying to take over Congress as well as the judiciary. Even New Deal supporters felt he was trying to "purge" the Democratic Party.

The result was that every man Roosevelt opposed was re-elected, except one representative from New York. In addition, the Republicans picked up seven seats in the Senate and 75 in the House. Perhaps if Louis Howe had been around to advise him, F.D.R. would have been less cocky and more cautious. But Howe had died in 1936 after a long illness.

To all intents and purposes, the 1938 congressional elections marked the end of the New Deal. After January 1939, no more major New Deal laws were passed. Those that had already been passed, however, changed the United States forever. Social Security, collective bargaining, rural electrification, the protection of bank deposits, and a minimum wage were just some of the changes that have become a permanent part of American life. Most citizens agreed with F.D.R. that it was indeed the business of government "to serve people and help them through crises beyond their control."

As it happens, another and different storm was looming on the horizon. Its two centers were the nations of Germany and Japan.

Chapter 9

Gathering Storm Clouds

E ver since his days as assistant secretary of the navy, F.D.R. had been concerned about world affairs. He believed that "when peace has been broken *anywhere*, the peace of all countries *everywhere* is in danger." He did not regard the Atlantic and Pacific oceans as walls behind which the United States could remain isolationist, with no concern about the rest of the world. Ever since he had first been elected President, Roosevelt had been trying to arouse the American people's interest in events in Europe and Asia. For his first six years in office, though, he had little success.

AGGRESSION IN THE PACIFIC

The Great Depression had not been limited just to the United States; it had affected nations all over the world. One of those that had been hardest hit was Japan. The collapse of world trade meant that Japan could no longer sell its rice, silk, and manufactured products abroad. As a result, it could not afford to buy the food and raw materials it needed from other nations. Japanese military leaders had been urging for some time that Japan establish an empire in Asia. As economic conditions within Japan worsened, more and more Japanese began agreeing with the military.

In 1931 Japan seized China's northeast province of Manchuria. Six years later, in 1937, it decided to try for all of China. Within a few months, Japanese armies overran almost the entire eastern half of the country.

Many Far Eastern experts believed Japan would not stop with China but would eventually try to take over the British, Dutch, and French colonies in the Pacific. These territories contained rich supplies of rubber, bauxite (aluminum ore), tin, and oil. The Philippine Islands, which belonged to the United States, were also believed to be on the Japanese agenda for conquest.

Most Americans, though, were not concerned about Japan—not even when Japanese planes bombed and sank a naval gunboat, the *U.S.S. Panay*, while it was escorting three oil tankers up the Yangtze River in China. The attack was clearly no accident. But when Japan apologized and offered to pay damages, most Americans simply gave a sigh of relief. After all, what did it really matter what was happening in far-off Asia? They had enough to worry about at home.

THE RISE OF NAZI GERMANY

On January 30, 1933, just five weeks before Roosevelt began his first term as President, Adolf Hitler was appointed chancellor of Germany. Unlike F.D.R., Hitler did not believe in democracy. Quite the contrary. He believed that ordinary people were incapable of governing themselves. What Germany needed was an absolute dictatorship under the National Socialist Workers' (Nazi) Party, with himself as *Der Fuhrer*, or the leader.

After receiving the power to suspend Germany's constitution and laws, Hitler began to turn the country into an armed camp. He believed that the "warrior [was] the noblest expression of the human spirit" and that Germany was destined to rule the world for a thousand years. Soon Germany was spending three-fourths of its national budget on armaments.

In addition to being anti-democratic and a militarist, Hitler was a racist. He considered Germans to be a "master race." He regarded Jews, Russians and other Slavs, and non-whites — except the Japanese — as inferior "races." They should either be turned into slaves to work for the Germans, he said, or they should be exterminated.

Most Americans, however, paid as little attention to Hitler's speeches and German rearmament as they did to Japan's war on China. They still felt the way they had at the end of World War I. Enough American boys had lost their lives because of Europe's internal quarrels. What the United States should do was to mind its own business. The Atlantic and Pacific oceans were enough to protect the country from Nazi and Japanese dictators. "America First!" they said.

CHALLENGING ISOLATIONISM

To Roosevelt, such ideas were unrealistic. In his mind, the United States had to be prepared to resist German and Japanese aggression. His problem was how to convince the American people.

Roosevelt first raised the issue publicly in a 1935 speech known as the "I-hate-war" speech. In it, he talked about his experiences in World War I and his hatred of war. Nevertheless, he argued, the country should be ready in case war came. Roosevelt felt that the United States needed to train more men for defense; spend more money to build battleships, tanks, and planes; and form alliances with other democratic nations. However, most Americans ignored the President's words. Preparing for war, they said, would only bring on war.

Later that year, Italy, an ally of Germany, invaded and conquered Ethiopia, a country in Africa. In March 1936, Hitler marched his troops into the Rhineland, a German area along the French border that was supposed to remain free of soldiers. That same month, an army revolt broke out against the government of Spain. The revolt was led by General Francisco Franco, who planned to set up a dictatorship. Both Germany and Italy promptly sent soldiers and weapons to help Franco's rebels. A few months later, Hitler and Italian dictator Benito Mussolini signed a military alliance known as the Rome-Berlin Axis.

In 1937 Roosevelt went to Chicago to dedicate the opening of a new bridge. While there, he delivered a second speech about the growing danger overseas.

"The peace, the freedom and the security of ninety percent of the population of the world is being jeopardized by the remaining ten percent who are threatening a breakdown of all international order and law," he pointed out. "When an epidemic of physical disease starts to spread, the community . . . joins in a quarantine of the patients in order to protect the health of the community against the spread of the disease." Aggressor nations, he continued, presented a similar threat to peace- and freedom-loving nations. The solution, he said, was to "quarantine the aggressors" through such actions as refusing to trade with them.

Once again, President Roosevelt's warning fell on deaf ears. Americans everywhere condemned him for "saber-rattling" and "war-mongering." "It's a terrible thing," F.D.R. commented sadly to a friend, "to look over your shoulder when you are trying to lead—and find no one there to follow you."

THE STORM ADVANCES

All through 1938 the threat of war grew stronger. In March Hitler invaded Austria and added its territory to that of the German Reich, or empire. In September he created a crisis over the Sudeten region of northern Czechoslovakia. Frightened at the idea of fighting, Great Britain and France agreed to let Hitler take over the Sudetenland in exchange for no more aggression. The British prime minister, Neville Chamberlain, asserted that his action had bought "peace in our time." Roosevelt, however, commented that when a police chief makes a deal with gangsters, he becomes nothing more than a member of their gang.

Roosevelt then sent a personal message to both Hitler and Mussolini. In it, he asked them to promise not to attack or invade other nations for a 10-year period. Mussolini simply ignored the message. Hitler read it aloud to his legislature, which burst into roars of laughter.

Still, American isolationists refused to worry. A man who sold peanuts outside the White House gate put it this way. "Over there, there are guns. Over here, there ain't no guns. Here there's squirrels on the lawn." Roosevelt agreed that the man was right. "But tell him that the fuss and pushing and guns in Europe are coming closer to our country all the time."

In March 1939, Hitler broke his promise not to seek more territory when he seized the rest of Czechoslovakia. The next month, Mussolini attacked Albania. On the other side of the world, Japan was making aggressive moves in the Pacific.

Roosevelt had previously asked Congress to repeal the Neutrality Acts of 1935, 1936, and 1937, which prohibited the United States from lending money or selling arms to warring nations. But Congress had turned him down. Now F.D.R. asked Congress to at least vote money for national defense. This time, Congress approved his request. Roosevelt also sent another personal appeal to Hitler and Mussolini, asking them to come to a peace conference and to "park their guns outside." The Axis powers responded by calling F.D.R.'s message a symptom of the "creeping paralysis that has attacked the President's mind."

A Royal Visit

In June 1939, F.D.R. enjoyed a pleasant interlude. He played host to King George VI and Queen Elizabeth of Great Britain. It was the first visit ever by a British monarch to the United States. Washington outdid itself. The capital glittered with flags and decorations, and people wore their fanciest clothes to the various receptions and balls.

After the official part of the visit was over, F.D.R. invited the royal couple to spend a weekend at Hyde Park. Sara Roosevelt was worried that the family mansion was not sufficiently elegant. It was not, after all, a castle. But the king and queen were delighted by the ease and informality of the First Family's home. And everyone enjoyed a picnic at which the king and queen had their first taste of such traditional American foods as hot dogs and strawberry shortcake.

That evening, the king and the President stayed up until one o'clock in the morning discussing national and international affairs. Just before they retired, King George said to F.D.R., "Why don't my ministers talk to me as you did tonight? I feel exactly as though a father were giving me his most careful and thoughtful advice."

THE STORM BREAKS

At 3:00 A.M. on the morning of September 1, 1939, the telephone at Roosevelt's bedside rang. He awoke with a start. It was William C. Bullitt, the American ambassador in Paris.

"Mr. President," said Bullitt, "several German divisions are deep in Polish territory. . . . There are reports of bombers over the city of Warsaw."

"Well, Bill," F.D.R. replied gravely, "it has come at last. God help us all!"

At 6:30 A.M., Bullitt called again. "Mr. President, I have talked with [the French premier]. He tells me France will go to Poland's aid." A few minutes later, Roosevelt heard from Joseph P. Kennedy, the American ambassador in London. "Britain will fight to help Poland," Kennedy reported.

Two days later, F.D.R. addressed the nation in a fireside chat. "Until four-thirty this morning," he said, "I had hoped against hope that some miracle would prevent a devastating war in Europe and bring to an end the invasion of Poland by Germany." But now, he told the American people, World War II had begun. Although he believed that "every battle that is fought does affect the American future," he promised his listeners that "this nation will remain a neutral nation." Nevertheless, he added, "Even a neutral has a right to take account of the facts. Even a neutral cannot be asked to close his mind or his conscience." It was clear which side the President was on.

Three weeks later, Roosevelt asked Congress to pass a new Neutrality Act. It would allow Great Britain and France to buy arms and ammunition on a "cash-and-carry" basis. That meant paying cash on delivery and carrying the goods from the United States to Europe in British and French ships. After much debate, Congress agreed.

BUILDING UP AMERICAN DEFENSES

The year 1940 was a disaster for Great Britain, France, and the other Allies. In April and May, Hitler's forces overwhelmed Denmark, Norway, Belgium, Luxembourg, and the Netherlands. In June Paris fell to the Nazis, and France surrendered. In August the Battle of Britain began. Night after night, as many as 1,000 German planes unleashed a torrent of bombs on London and other English cities. In the meantime, the Rome-Berlin Axis was joined by Japan.

Roosevelt found himself walking a tightrope. On the one hand, he was aware that only Great Britain stood between the United States and eventual Axis aggression. On the other hand, isolationist feelings in this country were still strong. Somehow, he had to persuade Congress and the people not only to build up America's defenses but also to support the Allies with "all aid short of war."

Roosevelt succeeded. In May he asked for and received congressional approval to build 50,000 combat planes a year. In July Congress voted funds for construction of a "two-ocean Navy." Until that time, the United States had relied on the British navy to patrol the Atlantic.

In September Roosevelt announced "a good horse trade." The United States had sent 50 over-age destroyers to Britain to use against Nazi submarines in the Atlantic. In exchange, the United States had received 99-year leases on eight British naval and air bases in the Western Hemisphere. Republicans and the press accused the President of being dictatorial and deceitful because he had not consulted Congress about the exchange. But F.D.R. pointed out that the U.S. Navy had the right to dispose of surplus property. He again stressed the importance of helping nations that by defending themselves were defending us. By this time, a poll showed that 60 percent of the American people agreed with Roosevelt.

In October Congress passed the first peacetime draft in the nation's history. Under the Selective Service Act, some 16 million Americans between ages 21 and 35 were to be registered for military training. Roosevelt acknowledged that the law was "a crushing blow for the fathers and mothers of this nation." But failure to pass it, he said, would have killed "our chances for survival."

The Manhattan Project

One of the results of Hitler's racial policies was that many Jewish scientists fled from Germany and Austria to seek refuge in the United States and Sweden. One of these scientists was Dr. Lise Meitner, who, late in 1938, realized the significance of certain laboratory experiments. Uranium atoms were being split, and each atom had the potential of releasing 20 million times as much energy as one atom of TNT.

Another refugee, Dr. Albert Einstein, believed the next step would be the development of a device to start uranium atoms splitting one after another in a chain reaction. The energy produced by this reaction could then be harnessed to build a weapon of unbelievable power. Einstein described his theory in a letter to Roosevelt in which he urged the President to explore nuclear power. It should be done quickly, Einstein added, because German scientists were also working on the idea.

Several of F.D.R.'s advisors discredited the suggestion. It was just some "crazy notion of a crackpot professor," they said. Roosevelt, however, did not want to take any chances. If Hitler was actually developing atomic weapons, then the United States must have them, too. He gave the go-ahead for a secret research project called the Manhattan Project. By 1945, it would produce the world's first atomic bomb.

THE THIRD-TERM CAMPAIGN

All during the spring of 1940, politicians whispered and wondered whether F.D.R. would run for a third term. No President had done so before. In fact, there was a strong tradition against it dating back to George Washington, who had declined a third term when it had been offered to him. Many people, however, pointed out that the Constitution did not limit a President to two terms. (The 22nd Amendment, which *does* limit the number of presidential terms, was not passed until 1951.) Moreover, they argued, Washington himself had said that a President could serve in an emergency as long as the people wanted him to. And there certainly was an emergency in 1940!

In June the Republicans nominated Wendell L. Willkie, an attractive and intelligent man. Although he had led the fight of public utility companies against the TVA, he supported other New Deal programs. He also agreed with F.D.R. that the United States could not remain isolationist.

Roosevelt was silent. He was almost 58 years old, and the idea of returning to Hyde Park and the Hudson Valley was very appealing. Even Eleanor was urging him not to run again. So he sounded out Secretary of State Cordell Hull to see if Hull was interested in the presidency, but Hull was not. The only other candidates were Vice-President Garner and Postmaster General Farley, but Roosevelt felt they lacked experience in foreign affairs. He was afraid that neither man would stand up to the Axis powers. So he let it be known that he would accept a draft—and the Democrats renominated him in July. Because Garner had opposed a third term, F.D.R. chose a new running mate for the vice-presidency: Secretary of Agriculture Henry A. Wallace.

A Nasty Fight

The 1940 presidential campaign was low and mean-spirited. Republicans accused the President of being a warmonger and a dictator, whose re-election would be "the last step in the destruction of our democracy." He was at the same time a "traitor to labor" and "the chief apostle of class hatred in the United States." Democrats mocked Willkie as "the barefoot boy of Wall Street." They whispered about his German ancestry and denounced him as "well-meaning, confused, and supported by Nazi agents." Republicans urged voters to strike F.D.R. out "at third." Democrats countered with the slogan "Better a Third-Termer than a Third-Rater."

At first Roosevelt stayed above it all, claiming that the rapid pace of events overseas made it necessary for him to remain close to the White House. However, as Willkie surged ahead in opinion polls, F.D.R. changed his mind. "I am an old campaigner, and I love a good fight."

Roosevelt launched into a full-scale attack on the Republican record in handling the Depression. "Back in 1932," he reminded voters, Republican leaders had been "willing to let workers starve if they could not get a job." They had "met the demands of unemployed veterans with troops and tanks." They had opposed unemployment insurance, a minimum wage, and collective bargaining. If the Republicans were now singing a different tune, F.D.R. observed sarcastically, "I wonder if the election could have something to do with it." As for foreign affairs, the President asserted, arming America was necessary in order to meet the inevitable Nazi challenge. At the same time, he promised voters that "Your boys are not going to be sent into any foreign wars."

Victory Yet Again

Almost 50 million people went to the polls on Election Day, the largest number ever. When the votes were counted, it was clear that the American people had chosen not to "change horses in the middle of the stream." Roosevelt's margin of victory was almost five million popular votes, while he swept the Electoral College by 449 to 82.

Surprisingly after such a vicious campaign, Willkie conceded defeat in a very statesmanlike speech. "Although constitutional government had been blotted out elsewhere," he said over the radio, "here in America men and women kept it triumphantly alive. No matter which side you were on, this great expression of faith in the free system of government must have given hope wherever man hopes to be free. . . . There is no bitterness in my heart; I hope there is none in yours. We have elected Franklin D. Roosevelt President. He is your President. He is my President. . . . And we will pray God may guide his hand during the next four years."

Willkie meant what he said. Soon he was working hard to develop Republican support for national defense and a bipartisan approach to foreign policy. It was to be sorely needed.

Chapter 10
The Road to War

Just before F.D.R.'s third inauguration, the President invited Chief Justice Charles Evans Hughes to dinner. The two men discussed arrangements for the swearing-in ceremony. "Mr. President," said Hughes, "after I have read the oath and you have repeated it, how would it do for me to lean forward and whisper: 'Don't you think this is getting just a little monotonous for both of us?' "

A SERIES OF SPEECHES

Roosevelt's third inaugural address was almost a call to arms. "In Washington's day the task of the people was to create and weld together a nation," he said. "In Lincoln's day the task of the people was to preserve that Nation from disruption from within. In this day," he asserted, "the task of the people is to save the Nation and its institutions from disruption from without."

The President sharply criticized those who believed that "tyranny and slavery have become the surging wave of the future—and that freedom is an ebbing tide." Just the opposite was true, he insisted. The proof lay in the fact that the

United States had fought the Depression without abandoning its democratic institutions.

Even before his inaugural address, F.D.R. had again urged the nation to meet the Axis challenge directly. In a fireside chat in December 1940, he proposed that the United States become "the great arsenal of democracy." It should supply food, weapons, and raw materials to those nations that were fighting the Axis threat.

LEND-LEASE

In his State of the Union address to Congress in January 1941, the President translated his idea for helping the Allies into concrete terms. Because he knew that Great Britain had no cash left to buy supplies under the existing cash-and-carry system, he asked Congress to pass the Lend-Lease Act. This act would give him the power to send military equipment to any nation whose defense he thought was vital to that of the United States. He could sell, transfer, exchange, lease, or lend such equipment.

Roosevelt related that if a neighbor wanted a garden hose to put out a fire, you wouldn't sell it to him, you would just expect him to bring it back. Opponents of the measure compared the Lend-Lease Act to lending someone chewing gum. Nobody would *want* it back. They also argued that the measure gave the President too much power. Willkie, however, strongly supported the idea, and the Lend-Lease Act was passed by Congress in March of 1941.

By May war supplies were piling up in American ports faster than they could be carried away in Allied ships. Ironically, the demand for weapons and munitions probably did more than the New Deal to end unemployment in the United States.

TROUBLES IN THE ATLANTIC

With the passage of the Lend-Lease Act, events moved rapidly. First, the United States set up military bases on Iceland and Greenland. Next, F.D.R. put factories to work building thousands of bombers. He also ordered the U.S. Navy to escort Allied supply ships part way across the Atlantic. But the destroyers did more than just serve as escorts. They located German submarines so that Allied warships could attack them.

When the Germans retaliated by torpedoing an American freighter, F.D.R. proclaimed an "unlimited national emergency." He ordered German and Italian consulates in the United States closed and told Nazi officials to leave the country. Then a German submarine fired on an American destroyer. F.D.R. responded by ordering American ships to "shoot on sight" any German submarines. By late fall of 1941, the United States was fighting an undeclared war in the Atlantic.

By this time, too, the Allies had been joined in the war against Germany by the Soviet Union. It was not a voluntary decision. In August 1939, Hitler had signed a nonaggression pact with Soviet dictator Joseph Stalin. When Germany invaded Poland from the west in September, the Soviet Union invaded it from the east. But after Hitler failed to bomb Britain into submission, he decided to turn his attention eastward. In June 1941, he broke his word and attacked the Soviet Union.

THE ATLANTIC CHARTER

For some time, Roosevelt had wanted to meet with the new British prime minister, Winston Churchill. Both men were, of course, extremely busy. However, in August 1941, they finally got together off the foggy coast of Newfoundland. For three days, meetings were held alternately on board the *U.S.S. Augusta* and the British *H.M.S. Prince of Wales*. Churchill hoped to persuade the United States to enter the war; Roosevelt wanted to plan for world peace after the war.

The two democratic leaders were soon calling each other by their first names. Clearly, although they disagreed on certain issues, they admired and respected each other. More important, both were aware that their nations had much in common and that if one fell, the other was doomed. The personal friendship between Roosevelt and Churchill was to have a profound effect on the conduct of World War II.

Another outcome of the meeting was the Atlantic Charter, which spelled out goals for a postwar world. The charter stated that neither the United States nor Great Britain wanted new territory. The two countries respected "the right of all people to choose the form of government under which they will live." They promised to help other countries improve their living conditions. And they looked forward to a world free from war and the burden of armaments.

TROUBLES IN THE PACIFIC

In the meantime, the situation on the other side of the world was becoming more threatening all the time. Soon after F.D.R. was elected President for the third time, he ordered Americans to stop selling scrap iron and steel to Japan. Then, in June 1941, the Dutch told the Japanese they could not buy oil from the Dutch East Indies (now Indonesia). These two actions cut off most of Japan's military raw materials. Frustrated, the Japanese decided they had no choice but to expand their war in the Pacific. When they sent their troops into southern Vietnam, the Allies feared that the next step was an invasion of Malaya, Singapore, and the Dutch East Indies.

Three battleships (from left to right: the West Virginia, Tennessee, and Arizona) burn following the Japanese attack on Pearl Harbor on December 7, 1941. The Arizona was totally destroyed (its sunken hulk is now a national memorial), but the other two ships were salvaged and later took part in naval battles. (U.S. Naval Institute.)

Roosevelt retaliated by cutting off all trade with Japan. In a series of talks with Secretary of State Cordell Hull, the Japanese ambassador tried to get the decision reversed. The Japanese also wanted the United States to stop sending Lend-Lease aid to China. The United States said it would—provided Japan withdrew its soldiers from both Vietnam and China.

In October the Japanese Cabinet resigned and a new Cabinet, consisting entirely of military men, was appointed in its place. Still, the talks between American and Japanese diplomats continued.

In November Roosevelt's Cabinet agreed to go to war if Japan launched any further attacks in Asia. Washington alerted American naval commanders in the Pacific to be ready for combat, and General Douglas MacArthur was ordered to strengthen the defenses of the Philippines. Nobody, however, thought the Japanese would strike where and when they did.

PEARL HARBOR

On Sunday afternoon, December 7, 1941, F.D.R. was working on his stamp collection. At 1:47 P.M., the telephone rang. It was Secretary of the Navy Frank Knox. He told Roosevelt that at 7:55 A.M. Hawaiian time, Japanese planes had attacked American territory—the U.S. naval base at Pearl Harbor. They had sunk or crippled six battleships, three destroyers, a number of other vessels, and 300 planes. They had also killed 2,403 Americans and wounded another 1,178. All this at a cost of only 29 Japanese planes. In addition, the Japanese had caught MacArthur's bombers on the ground in the Philippines and destroyed almost every one.

American neutrality was over. Like it or not, ready or not, the United States was at war.

Chapter 11

Commander-in-Chief

O n December 8, 1941, the White House—like the rest of the country—went on a war footing. Outdoor lights were turned off, black-out curtains were placed over all the windows, and the basement of the nearby Treasury Department was converted into an air raid shelter. Roosevelt jokingly told Secretary of the Treasury Morgenthau, "Henry, I will not go down into the shelter unless you allow me to play poker with all the gold in your vaults." White House residents and staff received gas masks, and gun crews took up positions on the White House roof.

WARTIME GOALS

On December 22 Winston Churchill arrived in Washington, where he and Roosevelt reached a major decision on military strategy. Because the Allies did not have enough soldiers and weapons to attack Germany and Japan at the same time, they would concentrate their efforts first against Hitler. Once they had secured victory in Europe, they would then turn their full attention to Japan.

On January 1, 1942, the 26 nations fighting Germany

signed the Declaration of the United Nations. (It was F.D.R. who suggested the name.) In the declaration, the nations — led by the United States, Great Britain, the Soviet Union, and China — promised to uphold the Atlantic Charter, fight with all their might, and never sign a separate peace.

On January 6 F.D.R. reinforced the declaration with a stirring call to the American people. "No compromise can end the conflict. There has never been, there can never be, successful compromise between good and evil. Only total victory can reward the champions of tolerance and decency and freedom and faith."

On February 5 Roosevelt delivered his first wartime State of the Union message to Congress. Again he spelled out the nation's goals. "Our own objectives are clear . . . smashing the militarism imposed by war lords upon their enslaved peoples . . . liberating the subjugated nations . . . establishing and securing freedom of speech, freedom of religion, freedom from want, and freedom from fear everywhere in the world." To F.D.R., the "Four Freedoms" were basic rights of humanity.

The President then announced his military production goals: 60,000 planes, 45,000 tanks, 20,000 antiaircraft guns, and six million tons of shipping. And that was just for 1942! Roosevelt wanted double those amounts produced in 1943. When Harry Hopkins, who was coordinating the war effort, commented that those were astronomical figures, F.D.R. replied with his usual optimism, "Oh, the production people can do it if they really try." Sure enough, they did.

WARTIME AGENCIES

Roosevelt applied the same organizational skills and flair for experiment to administering the war as he had to running the New Deal. Under his direction, a whole series of wartime agencies, commonly known as the "alphabetocracy," were established.

The War Production Board indicated which plants were to convert from peacetime to wartime production, while the Board of Economic Warfare stockpiled supplies. The War Manpower Commission supervised employment; the National War Labor Board regulated wages, hours, and working conditions; and the War Food Administration directed the nation's food program.

The result of all these wartime agencies was an avalanche of goods. American factories operated 24 hours a day turning out the thousands of items needed in modern warfare. American workers set one production record after another, such as building a Liberty Ship (freighter) in 41 days instead of the usual 242 days. American farmers fed not only our own armed forces and population but a large part of the world as well.

Nor did F.D.R. neglect the home front. He remembered how prices had skyrocketed during World War I, hurting many people. To prevent this from happening again, he set up the Office of Price Administration. The OPA fixed maximum rents and set top prices on goods. It also established a rationing system for items such as meat, butter, sugar, coffee, tires, and gasoline that were needed by the armed forces. People could buy these goods only if they had stamps from ration books.

RUNNING THE MILITARY

Roosevelt also reorganized the military. He combined the different army bureaus into three main groups—ground force, air force, and supply—and placed General George C. Marshall at their head as Chief of Staff. Naval operations were divided between an Atlantic fleet and a Pacific fleet.

Perhaps the most significant fact was that F.D.R. trusted his commanders. After he had set the overall strategy, such as deciding to defeat Germany ahead of Japan, he then allowed his commanders to carry it out without interference. He was also quick to understand such aspects of modern warfare as the importance of air power. For example, in May of 1942, American ships won the battle of the Coral Sea against Japanese ships using only carrier-based airplanes. Not a single shot was fired by one battleship against another. In fact, the two fleets did not even come within sight of each other. Roosevelt immediately stopped the construction of any more battleships and had existing ones converted into aircraft carriers.

MAINTAINING MORALE

Part of the task of being a wartime leader was keeping up the spirits of the American people. At this, Roosevelt was superb. If there were no victories he could describe in his fireside chats—and there were none at first—he told stories about individual acts of heroism by American fighting men and women. He visited the wounded in hospitals, cracking jokes as his wheelchair was rolled through the wards.

One of F.D.R.'s favorite stories was about a marine on the Pacific island of Guadalcanal. The marine was unhappy because he had not killed any Japanese, who were concealed in the jungle. His superior officer advised him to go up on a hill and shout, "To hell with Emperor Hirohito!" That was bound to bring the Japanese out of hiding. The marine did as he had been told, and at once a Japanese soldier came out of the jungle shouting, "To hell with Roosevelt!" "And of course," said the marine, "I could not shoot a fellow Republican."

Actually, just seeing F.D.R. in person made a big difference to the wounded. After all, he knew from personal experience how discouraging it was to face a sudden physical handicap. Yet there he was, the President of the United States, with a broad grin on his face and an unquenchable determination in his voice.

In a different vein, F.D.R. remembered how bitter many of the veterans returning from World War I had been over the interruption in their lives. Because he wanted to avoid a similar situation after World War II, in 1944 he asked Congress to pass the so-called G.I. Bill of Rights. Under this law, the federal government agreed to pay tuition for those veterans who wanted to attend college or technical school. In that way they could make up for the education they had missed while in service. Also, if veterans wanted to buy a house or a farm, or set up a business, the federal government promised to guarantee bank loans for such purposes at low interest rates. The result of the G.I. Bill was that almost eight million veterans went to school at government expense after the war ended, while millions of young families became proud owners of houses, farms, and businesses they probably could not have otherwise afforded.

THE WARTIME CONFERENCES

In addition to inspiring people at home, F.D.R. spent considerable time meeting and negotiating with America's allies. It took all his political skill. Some of the Allied leaders — especially Chiang Kai-shek (now spelled Jiang Jieshi) of China and General Charles de Gaulle of France — had difficult personalities. And all of them had their own interests. It was hard getting them to work together for the common good.

The Casablanca Conference

On January 9, 1943, Roosevelt flew to Casablanca, Morocco, to meet Churchill. It was the first time he had flown since his trip to Chicago in 1932 to accept the presidential nomination. It was also the first time a President had left the United States during wartime.

At Casablanca the two leaders discussed further strategy. They planned the invasion of the European continent through its "soft underbelly" of Sicily and Italy. They also decided to reopen the Burma Road across the Himalaya Mountains so that China could receive needed supplies. And they announced that the Allies would not negotiate peace with the Axis powers but would insist on "unconditional surrender."

While at the conference, F.D.R. had a chance to see two of his sons: Lieutenant Colonel Elliott Roosevelt, who was a reconnaissance pilot, and Lieutenant Franklin D. Roosevelt, Jr., who was serving on a destroyer in the Mediterranean. Roosevelt's two other sons and his son-in-law also were in combat, for the President refused to use his position as Commander-in-Chief to protect family members. In his opinion, every American was in the struggle on the same basis.

The Teheran Conference

The next major international conference between F.D.R. and Churchill took place in November 1943 at Teheran, Iran. Soviet leader Joseph Stalin also attended this conference, which was the first time F.D.R. and Stalin had met. The President found the Russian dictator to be somber, suspicious, and iron-willed. Roosevelt turned on all his charm and by the end of the conference was addressing Stalin as "Uncle Joe." Unfortunately, F.D.R. apparently believed that Stalin was simply a Russian version of a tough Democratic political boss. He

Roosevelt confers with General Dwight Eisenhower (right) at an airport in Sicily during a stopover on the way to the Teheran Conference. (Franklin D. Roosevelt Library.)

did not fully appreciate the fact that Stalin had risen to power, not by elections and political deals, but by treachery and murder.

This first conference of the "Big Three" laid plans for a second front in Europe. It was decided that in June 1944, a million men under the command of American General

Dwight D. Eisenhower would strike at Germany. Allied troops would cross the English Channel from England and land on the Normandy coast of France. Meanwhile, the Russian Army would invade Germany through Poland. Another long-range decision was a promise by Stalin that six months after Germany surrendered, he would declare war on Japan. The six-month interval was to give the Soviet Union time to move its armies from Europe to Asia.

Roosevelt was not satisfied, however. Now that the Allies had planned how to end the war, he wanted to plan the peace as well. As a strong supporter of the League of Nations after World War I, F.D.R. now argued with all his might that the United States, Great Britain, the Soviet Union, and China jointly take the lead in setting up a world organization to keep the peace.

Neither Churchill nor Stalin were as idealistic as Roosevelt. Nor did they know that the United States was developing the atom bomb. To F.D.R., the development of nuclear weapons meant that nations either had to get along with one another or face mutual extermination.

In the end, the Teheran conferees settled for an uplifting statement without any details. Roosevelt, however, felt that an important step had been taken toward transforming the wartime alliance into a peacetime alliance. In August his hopes were borne out. Diplomats from the four leading Allied nations met at Washington, D.C., and drafted a preliminary Charter of the United Nations.

SOME DOMESTIC AND FOREIGN FAILURES

Despite Roosevelt's momentous achievements at home and abroad, there were two areas in which his actions did not measure up to his beliefs. One had to do with the treatment of Americans of Japanese descent; the other with the failure of the United States to take steps to save European Jews from extermination in Hitler's death camps.

Interning the Japanese-Americans

Many people living on the West Coast had never liked the Japanese-Americans who also lived there. Their appearance and religion differed from those of the majority, and they were also successful farmers and business people. Soon after the attack on Pearl Harbor, stories began circulating that lights had been seen flashing from coastal homes. Obviously, the Japanese-Americans were traitors who were signaling the Japanese fleet.

On February 19, 1942, President Roosevelt ordered the army to round up persons who were considered a threat to national security. About 112,000 Japanese-Americans, of whom two-thirds were citizens, were uprooted from their homes and businesses and sent to internment camps, most of which were located in the deserts of California and Arizona. As a show of loyalty, despite the way they and their families had been treated, all the young men from the camps enlisted in the American armed forces and fought bravely in Europe. None of the interred Japanese-Americans were ever charged with spying or sabotage, yet they remained behind barbed wire until after the end of the war.

Rejecting the Jews

By 1942 Roosevelt began receiving reports about the systematic murder of Jews in Nazi death camps. As the toll mounted into the millions, Jewish organizations in the United States appealed to the President to do something—anything.

The Nazis were willing to release small numbers of Jews

in exchange for money. Would F.D.R. negotiate the matter with Hitler? Some Jews were managing to escape from Nazi Germany. Would F.D.R. suspend American immigration quotas—which were not being used in any event—and admit refugees to this country? Every day, railroad cars carried thousands of Jews to the death camps. Would Roosevelt order the U.S. Air Force to bomb German railroad lines so as to keep the trains from running? Would he order bombs dropped on the gas chambers in which the Jews were being murdered?

Roosevelt did none of these things. It is easy to understand his unwillingness to negotiate with Hitler. It is much harder to understand why he refused to suspend immigration quotas, or why he did not divert American bombers to attack Germany's railroads and death camps when they were already bombing German cities. It was not until 1944 that F.D.R. finally set up a War Refugee Board. Despite footdragging by the State Department, the board succeeded in saving about 50,000 out of six million Nazi victims.

GOOD NEWS FROM THE WAR FRONT

By the fall of 1944, the United States and its allies were well on the road to victory over the Axis.

On June 6 the strategy that F.D.R. had helped work out at Teheran was put into effect. The largest amphibious force ever assembled struck the Normandy coast on "D" Day. That evening, the President went on the air to lead the American people in a special prayer he had written:

> Almighty God: Our sons . . . this day have set upon a mighty endeavor, a struggle to preserve our Republic, our religion, and our civilization, and to set free a suffering humanity. . . . They fight not for the lust of conquest. . . . They fight to liberate. . . . They yearn but for the end of battle, for their re-

turn to the haven of home. Some will never return. Embrace these, Father, and receive them, Thy heroic servants, into Thy Kingdom.

The Allied troops began pushing the Germans back. In the Pacific theater, American bombers started large-scale air attacks against Japan. Also, American ground forces captured such islands as Saipan and Guam, thereby opening up a path to Japan itself. In October one of the greatest sea battles in history, the Battle of Leyte Gulf, was fought off the Philippines. When it was over, the American fleet controlled the Pacific. By this time, General Douglas MacArthur had returned to the Philippines in triumph, and Japan's prime minister had resigned in disgrace.

THE LAST PRESIDENTIAL CAMPAIGN

In July 1944 the Democrats nominated Roosevelt for a fourth term. He really did not want the nomination. For one thing, his health was declining. In January he caught a bad case of the flu, causing Eleanor to write a relative that "F.D.R. says he feels much better but I don't think he longs to get back and fight." All through the spring, he suffered from a low-grade fever that came and went. By early summer, the stresses of his job had brought about a heart condition, and a heart specialist was now always at his side. The tremendous energy and robust strength of earlier years were gone.

Doing His Duty

Then, too, F.D.R. was lonely. Sara Roosevelt had died in 1941, his four sons were in the armed forces, and Eleanor was usually away touring military bases and war plants. His secretary, Missy LeHand, and the Reverend Endicott Peabody both died in 1944. The only bright spots were dinners with Lucy Mercer Rutherford, who had been widowed a few years before.

However, F.D.R. felt that he could not give up when there was still a job to be done. Although the war itself was going well, many postwar issues remained to be worked out. So one week before the Democratic National Convention, Roosevelt wrote to the party's chairman: "All that is in me cries out to go back to my home on the Hudson River, but we of this generation chance to live in a day and hour when our Nation has been attacked, and when its future existence and the future existence of our chosen method of government are at stake. . . . As a good soldier . . . I will accept and serve." Because southerners and party officials considered Vice-President Wallace too liberal, F.D.R. chose as his new running mate Senator Harry S. Truman of Missouri.

A Change in Strategy

At first F.D.R. intended to stay off the campaign trail. He did not want America's wartime unity to be split by a partisan fight. Also, the Republican candidate—New York Governor Thomas E. Dewey—was young and vibrant. Roosevelt was aware that he himself looked gray and gaunt in comparison.

The Republicans, however, again waged a vicious personal campaign against F.D.R. They referred to the war as "Roosevelt's war." They said the President was unpatriotic because some of his advisors were "foreign-born" and probably either communists or at least communist sympathizers. They also whispered that F.D.R. was so ill that he could no longer function effectively.

By August F.D.R. realized that he would have to change his campaign strategy. He began by making "nonpartisan" inspection tours of naval bases and other military installations. He also made hundreds of stops along the way to grin and wave at the people so they could see that he was still fit to run the country.

The "Fala" Speech

In addition, F.D.R. delivered a number of witty, effective campaign speeches. The most outstanding speech had to do with Fala, the newest in a long succession of Scottish terriers. A lively, affectionate animal, Fala and the President were inseparable. The dog attended press conferences and Cabinet meetings, sat by the White House pool while F.D.R. went swimming, and slept on a blanket in the President's bedroom. When F.D.R. went riding in his open car, there was Fala on the seat beside him. When F.D.R. traveled to Hyde Park, Fala did, too. He even accompanied his master on sea voyages.

It was while on one such voyage to Alaska that a Republican congressman accused F.D.R. of leaving Fala behind on an island and then sending a U.S. Navy destroyer back to pick up the animal. Roosevelt's voice was solemn as he discussed the accusation before a campaign audience. "These Republican leaders have not been content with attacks—on me, or my wife, or on my sons," he said. "No, not content with that, they now include my little dog, Fala. Well, of course, I don't resent attacks, and my family doesn't resent attacks, but Fala *does* resent them."

Roosevelt went on to explain why. "You know—Fala's Scotch, and being a Scottie, as soon as he learned that the Republican fiction writers in Congress and out had concocted a story that I left him behind on an Aleutian Island and had sent a destroyer back to find him—at a cost to the taxpayers of two or three, or eight or twenty million dollars—his Scotch soul was furious. He has not been the same dog since." The

Presidential Pets

Ever since the days of Thomas Jefferson, the White House has been home to a wide variety of presidential pets. The most common have been dogs and horses. Next have come birds—ranging from Jefferson's mockingbird to William McKinley's Mexican double-yellow-headed parrot.

William Howard Taft was the last President to keep a cow—Pauline Wayne by name. Actually, cows were a necessity before the 20th century, for there were no dairy companies to deliver fresh milk. The milk produced by White House cows was stored in marble vats in the White House basement. The cook used a special ladle to skim off the cream.

Also popular until recent times were goats. When President Benjamin Harrison was a child, he loved to ride around the White House grounds in a red wagon pulled by a billy goat belonging to his grandfather, President William Henry Harrison. Naturally, one of the pets President Benjamin Harrison had was a billy goat to pull *his* grandchildren's wagon around.

In a more patriotic vein were the flock of 13 sheep and a tobacco-chewing ram named Old Ike that were owned by President Woodrow Wilson. During World War I, Americans were urged to conserve materials and labor. So the President decided that the best way to keep the White House lawn trimmed without extra gardeners was by keeping sheep. Unfortunately, the animals ate not

> only the grass but also the shrubs and
> flowers. On the other hand, their wool was
> auctioned off and the money given to the Red
> Cross. It is estimated that the wool from Wil-
> son's sheep brought in $100,000.

audience roared with laughter, and the incident undoubtedly helped Roosevelt win re-election to a fourth term.

Fourth-Term President

The final vote was the closest of F.D.R.'s four presidential races. Roosevelt's winning margin was 25,606,585 votes to Dewey's 22,014,745 votes. The Electoral College, however, was more lopsided: 432 to 99.

Soon after his victory, Roosevelt went to Warm Springs for a rest. It was only the third time he had been there since the United States entered the war. By January 1945, he was back in Washington.

Chapter 12

The Final Days

R oosevelt's fourth inauguration was very different from the other three. Despite Allied victories, millions of Americans were still fighting overseas, and the public mood was somber. So there was no parade on Inauguration Day, and the swearing-in ceremony—held at the White House instead of at the Capitol—was brief.

Roosevelt himself looked tired and haggard. He had lost a considerable amount of weight, and his eyes "were ringed and puffed with age." Nevertheless, he spelled out his hopes for the future with his usual determination and optimism.

"We can and we will achieve . . . a just and honorable peace, a durable peace," he asserted. ". . . We have learned that we cannot live alone, at peace; that our own well-being is dependent on the well-being of other nations far away. We have learned," he continued, "that we must live as men, not as ostriches, nor as dogs in the manger. We have learned to be citizens of the world, members of the human community."

THE YALTA CONFERENCE

At the end of January 1945, F.D.R. left Washington for Yalta, in the Russian Crimea, to take part in the second "Big Three" conference. The President's main objective at the conference was to get the Soviet Union to enter the struggle against Japan as quickly as possible.

Roosevelt appeared tired at the Yalta Conference. As Commander-in-Chief of the U.S. Navy, he often wore the dark blue cape of a naval officer. (Franklin D. Roosevelt Library.)

Roosevelt's advisors, including General MacArthur, believed the war in the Pacific could not be won until the end of 1946. The atom bomb had not yet been tested, which meant the Allies would have to invade the Japanese home islands. In light of the fact that Japanese pilots were killing themselves by deliberately crashing their planes into American naval vessels and that Japanese soldiers usually fought to the death, such an invasion—in the judgment of the military—would probably result in 1.5 million Allied casualties. The sooner Stalin joined in, the better.

In exchange, Roosevelt and Churchill agreed to several political concessions in Eastern Europe. As a result of these concessions, Communist governments were established in several nations there. The Soviets also received some Japanese territory.

The Big Three also reached several agreements about Germany. After the war, the country was to be temporarily divided into American, British, French, and Soviet zones. This agreement led to the eventual formation of two German nations, commonly known as West Germany and East Germany. Other items on the Yalta agenda included the break-up of Germany's industrial plants, German reparations, and the creation of a special international court to try some Nazis as war criminals.

An international peace-keeping organization had always been close to F.D.R.'s heart. At Yalta, Stalin agreed to join the United Nations, the first meeting of which would be held at San Francisco on April 25.

Reporting to Congress

All in all, F.D.R. was pleased with the results of the Yalta Conference. He was especially hopeful about the United Nations. As he explained to Congress on March 1: "[After World War I,] American fighting men looked to the statesmen of the world to finish the work of peace for which they fought and suffered. We failed them. We failed them then. We cannot fail them again, and expect the world to survive."

Roosevelt's speech was warmly received, but many members of Congress were shocked by the President's appearance. His face was pale and thin. His voice was no longer vibrant, and he rambled while he spoke. Furthermore, F.D.R. delivered his speech sitting down. "I hope you will pardon me for the unusual posture of sitting down during the presentation of what I want to say," he started out, "but I know you will realize it makes it a lot easier for me in not having to carry about ten pounds of steel around the bottom of my legs; and

also because I have just completed a 14,000-mile trip." It was
the first time F.D.R. had said anything in public about the
infantile paralysis that had crippled him 24 years before.

THE LAST TRIP TO WARM SPRINGS

Following the speech, Roosevelt went to Warm Springs at his
doctor's orders for "a period of total rest." After a few days
in the warm sun, F.D.R. began to look and feel better. He
read the newspapers, answered mail, and received visitors.
He began writing a speech to be delivered over the radio on
Jefferson Day, April 13. He looked forward to being in San
Francisco for the opening session of the United Nations on
April 25.

On Thursday, April 12, F.D.R. was working on his stamp
collection in the living room of the Little White House. With
him were two cousins, including the one who had given him
Fala. Also present was Lucy Mercer Rutherford.

Around noon, an artist named Elizabeth Shoumatoff arrived to do a portrait of F.D.R. that Lucy had commissioned.
As the artist sketched away, F.D.R. read some documents.
Suddenly he pressed his hand to his forehead. "I have a ter-
rific headache," he murmured. His head dropped forward and
he slumped unconscious in his chair. A doctor was summoned
immediately, but to no avail. The President died a few hours
later without regaining consciousness.

The official bulletin announced simply: "ARMY-NAVY
DEAD: Roosevelt, Franklin D., Commander in Chief." The
cause of death was a cerebral hemorrhage—a broken blood
vessel in the brain.

The next morning, the President's coffin was placed on
a funeral train as Chief Petty Officer Graham Jackson played
"Going Home" on the accordion. Millions of sorrowful peo-

The nation mourned as Franklin D. Roosevelt's body was carried through the streets of Washington on a flag-covered cart pulled by horses. (Franklin D. Roosevelt Library.)

ple lined the railroad tracks in Georgia, the Carolinas, and Virginia to wave good-bye to their fallen leader. After a state funeral procession in Washington, the flag-draped coffin was carried up the Hudson Valley and buried in the rose garden at Hyde Park.

Among the papers Roosevelt left on his desk in Warm Springs was the draft of his Jefferson Day speech. It closed with words typical of F.D.R.'s lifelong attitude: "The only limit to our realization of tomorrow will be our doubts of today. Let us move forward with strong and active faith."

Bibliography

Hacker, Jeffrey H. *Franklin D. Roosevelt.* New York: Franklin Watts, 1983. An extremely informative biography that stresses the political underpinnings and significance of Roosevelt's actions.

Hickok, Lorena A. *The Road to the White House.* Philadelphia and New York: Chilton Books, 1962. An intimate, well-written account of the pre-presidential years of F.D.R. that emphasizes how his character was shaped by his early life.

Johnson, Gerald W. *Franklin D. Roosevelt.* New York: William Morrow, 1967. A well-written biography that focuses on Roosevelt's personality.

McKown, Robin. *Roosevelt's America.* New York: Grosset & Dunlap, 1962. The highlights of F.D.R.'s life are presented against a detailed, extensively illustrated background of developments in such fields as sports, inventions, fashions, movies, and the like. Easy reading.

Meltzer, Milton. *Brother, Can You Spare a Dime?* New York: New American Library, 1969. A vivid account of the Great Depression from 1929 to 1933, containing numerous personal stories, songs, and prints and photographs of the period.

Peare, Catherine Owens. *The FDR Story.* New York: Thomas Y. Crowell, 1962. A pleasantly written, comprehensive biography, with considerable information about F.D.R.'s war against polio.

Sullivan, Wilson. *Franklin Delano Roosevelt.* New York: American Heritage, 1970. Well-written and lavishly illustrated with cartoons and drawings as well as photographs, this biography combines a detailed account of Roosevelt's political achievements with numerous incidents of his private life.

Thomas, Henry. *Franklin Delano Roosevelt.* New York: G. P. Putnam's, 1962. A somewhat partisan, easy-to-read biography filled with anecdotes.

Werstein, Irving. *A Nation Fights Back.* New York: Julian Messner, 1962. An exciting, fast-moving description of the Great Depression, including the events that led up to it as well as its aftermath. Contains many quotations from the period.

Index